THE STORY OF
BRADFORD

THE STORY OF
BRADFORD

ALAN HALL

The History Press

For my son Robert

First published 2013

The History Press
The Mill, Brimscombe Port
Stroud, Gloucestershire, GL5 2QG
www.thehistorypress.co.uk

© Alan Hall, 2013

The right of Alan Hall to be identified as the Author
of this work has been asserted in accordance with the
Copyright, Designs and Patents Act 1988.

British Library Cataloguing in Publication Data.
A catalogue record for this book is available from the British Library.

ISBN 978 0 7524 9977 2

Typesetting and origination by The History Press
Printed in Great Britain

CONTENTS

ACKNOWLEDGEMENTS

I am very grateful to Sue Naylor, who is responsible for many of the fine photographs in this book, including all of the colour photographs (unless otherwise stated). Sue also sourced copies of photographs from bygone years. I am also grateful to the staff of Bradford Central Library, especially Sue Caton, who patiently answered my queries, provided books and articles for me to study and helped locate photographs from the library's impressive photographic archive. I want to thank those writers and copyright-holders who kindly gave their blessing for certain source material to be used. Thanks must also go to my wife Mandy for encouraging me to write the book. She also read through parts of the text, pointing out errors and making valuable suggestions.

All proceeds from *The Story of Bradford* will go to Bradford Civic Society.

INTRODUCTION

The story of Bradford is of a place which was really of only local significance until the nineteenth century, at which point it underwent a quite remarkable expansion in size and importance until, by the end of the century, it had become a major city and achieved worldwide recognition. Immediately before the First World War it was estimated by some to be the wealthiest city in Europe, although of course that wealth was by no means evenly spread throughout the populace.

If in the late nineteenth and early twentieth centuries Bradford was renowned for its textile trade, in the second half of the twentieth century it became just as well known for the large numbers of people from all over the world who came to start new lives in the city. Observers and decision-makers throughout the UK (and beyond) have often looked closely at Bradford to see how it was coping with the challenges – and the opportunities – that this great influx of newcomers has presented.

One fascinating thread which runs through the story of Bradford from the earliest times right up to the present day is a tradition of dissent and rebelliousness. As far back as the Roman period the local Celtic people, members of the Brigantes tribe, never really accepted their occupation by a foreign power. The Angles and Scandinavian inhabitants of the region always wanted to be independent of the Saxons of southern England. Later they suffered cruelly for rebelling against William the Conqueror. At the time of the English Civil War, a few centuries later, Bradford was a town populated by a very independently-minded people who were not prepared to put up with the arbitrary rule of King Charles, nor with any attempts to stifle their Puritan form of worship.

Again, one of the characteristic features of the textile barons of the nineteenth century was that the majority of them were Nonconformists in their religion and Liberal in their politics, rather than being Tory members of the upper class and adherents of the established Church of England. Not that these wealthy manufacturers always had things their own way. From time to time the workers of Bradford rebelled, bitter strikes took place and troops with fixed-bayonets were sometimes required to restore order. And in more recent times, while we might be appalled by their actions, there is no doubt that the rioters who took to Bradford's streets in 1995 and 2001 were in their own way showing their dissent and challenging the authorities – just as others in Bradford have done down the centuries.

This particular story of Bradford deals mainly with the city as it was defined before the boundary changes of 1974. After that year Bradford expanded to become the City of Bradford Metropolitan District, taking in towns and villages that to a large extent had previously run their own affairs. In truth many of the inhabitants of these places preferred it that way, and they have often rather strongly resented being incorporated into Bradford – ask anyone from Ilkley or Keighley! However, the story of Bradford is in part also the story of these communities. It would be foolish, for example, to ignore Titus Salt's model township, or leave the Brontë sisters out of the story just because Haworth and Saltaire were technically outside Bradford's boundaries until comparatively recently. Like it or not, they are part of Bradford now, and in terms of political or economic dependence they probably always were.

A complete history of Bradford would run to several volumes. These fifteen short chapters necessarily omit some parts of the story and give only a helicopter camera's view of other parts. And as the book is essentially for the general reader it is not cluttered with in-depth notes and detailed references to sources, such as might appear in a more specialist work aimed at the professional historian. There is a bibliography of recommended reading, however, and I am grateful to all the writers of the books listed for the information and inspiration they have provided to enable me to tell the story of Bradford.

one

EARLY TIMES

Until the early years of the twenty-first century, just across the River Aire from Saltaire, was a public house with a curious name, the Cup and Ring. The name has nothing to do with drinking vessels or boxing matches; rather it alludes to a collection of boulders with strange markings that can be found a couple of miles away at the edge of Baildon Moor, quite near to Baildon Golf Club. Nobody has offered a completely satisfactory explanation of what these stones signify, nor how long they have been there, although the consensus is that they probably date from the early Bronze Age and possibly had a religious significance. Such cup and ring stones are not unique to the Bradford area; they can be found in other places in the North of England and also in parts of Scotland. Baildon Moor also contains several burial mounds from the Bronze Age, and some axes believed to be from this period have been found in the locality. Flint arrow-heads, probably from an earlier period, have also been found on Baildon Moor and in other parts of Bradford, notably Thornton, West Bowling and Eccleshill.

Celtic tribes migrated from mainland Europe to Britain from about 500 BC onwards, and these were the people that the Romans encountered when they began to colonise the country after AD 43. With the exception of the so-called swastika stone on Ilkley Moor, another boulder with unexplained markings but believed to be of Celtic origin, there is scant evidence of a Celtic presence in the Bradford area. Roman coins from the first and the fourth century AD have, however, been found in various places throughout Bradford, including Heaton, Idle and Cottingley, indicating the possibility that local Celtic people traded with the Roman occupiers, or used the coins for commercial activities between themselves.

It has to be said that these archaeological finds, especially when compared with what has been unearthed in other parts of Britain, do not amount to very much. This would seem to show that Bradford and its environs were rather off the beaten track. There was a Roman fort at Ilkley – called Olicana – but it was relatively small, and its prime function was to safeguard communications across the Pennines and keep the local population under control. There is no evidence that any Romans ever set foot in the bowl-shaped valley that was to become the centre of the city of Bradford; there was no real reason for them to do so. They may have had dealings with the primitive iron industry that existed at Bierley, as Roman coins have been found at this site, but this does not necessarily mean that any Romans actually visited the place.

Celtic people in the area would almost certainly be members of the Brigantes tribe who inhabited a large part of the North of England and were never com-pletely subjugated by the Romans. We do not know to what extent, if any, local

Bronze Age Cup and Ring stones, Baildon Moor. (Sue Naylor)

people were involved when the Brigantes revolted against the Romans in the first and third centuries AD. In short, with the exception of Olicana, the Roman occupation of Britain largely passed the Bradford area by.

Angles and Scandinavians

The Romans left Britain in the early part of the fifth century AD and between then and the Norman Conquest the country was subjected to successive waves of immigrants from what is now Germany and Scandinavia. Older histories often took the line that the Celtic inhabitants of Britain were forced west-wards *en masse* into Wales and Cornwall by these incoming peoples; modern historians tend to believe that, while there were episodes of conflict, such as the Battle of Catterick in AD 600, in the longer term the newcomers and the

Celts probably intermarried, and the reason that the western extremities of Britain remained predominantly Celtic was simply because the Anglo-Saxons never settled those areas in any numbers. The particular people who settled in what was to become West Yorkshire were the Angles, who are believed to have migrated from what is now Schleswig-Holstein in northern Germany. It is likely that they assimilated the Celts rather than driving them away. And the same process was probably repeated when the Norse people, or Vikings, arrived in the area in the ninth and tenth centuries.

The barbaric and bloodthirsty reputation of the Vikings owes much to their portrayal in the *Anglo-Saxon Chronicle*, which was written by Christian monks who naturally felt antagonistic towards the pagan Norsemen. In fact the Vikings established a flourishing independent territory – the Danelaw – in the North of England, with its capital at Jorvik (York). They eventually converted to Christianity and, once established on the land, were unlikely to have been particularly hostile to their Angle neighbours. Their hostility was more likely to have been directed towards the Saxons of southern England who constantly sought to dominate them and take away their independence, right up to the time of the Norman Conquest. Viewed in this light, Alfred the Great, King of Wessex, is not so much a national hero for people in the North of England, but rather an oppressor of their forebears.

Again, archaeological remains from this whole period are very few in the Bradford area, but at least it is possible to tell something about how the land was settled by a study of local place names. Thus the Anglo-Saxon ending *-ton*, as in Thornton, Clayton and Allerton, indicates an enclosure, while the very common ending *-ley*, as in Keighley and Bingley, indicates a clearing in woodland. It is easy to deduce from this that Skipton originally meant an enclosure for sheep and Shipley meant a clearing for sheep. There is evidence of Norse settlements too in place names like Micklethwaite, near Bingley. Denholme may indicate a Danish settlement, although *den* is also the Anglo-Saxon word for a small valley (modern English dean or dene). Bradford itself derives its name from the words for broad and ford and refers to a settlement that was established at a crossing point on a tributary of the River Aire. The ford was almost certainly in the vicinity of today's Forster Square.

Angle and Scandinavian influences can also be seen right up to the present in the way many people from West Yorkshire speak. Local people typically use short vowels and a rather flat intonation, making their speech sound quite different from that of southern England, which was mainly populated by the Saxons.

Southern English had much less linguistic input from Scandinavia. Many words that have their origins in Denmark and Norway are still in common use in West Yorkshire. Instead of hill-walking local people will walk the *fells* and *dales* (valleys), perhaps stopping to cool their feet not in a stream but a *beck*, before refreshing themselves with some *ale* while watching their *barns* (children) *laiking* (playing) or *ligging* (lying down) on the grass to rest. Even *ta*, often wrongly dismissed as a slang or infantile word, is cognate with the modern Danish word *tak*, which is the word for thanks.

The Norman Conquest

The people of the North of England did not readily accept England's new Norman rulers after the Conquest of 1066. Three years later there was an uprising, which King William crushed by laying waste large areas of land north of the Humber. This was the so-called Harrying of the North. The entry in the Domesday Book of 1086 shows that the manor of Bradford was itself laid waste: 'In Bradeford with six berewicks, Gamel had fifteen caracutes of land to be taxed, where there may be eight ploughs. Ilbert has it and it is waste. Value in King Edward's time four pounds.' In more modern parlance this means that in the manor of Bradford there were eight ploughs belonging to the lord of the manor to cultivate about 1,600 acres, and that the local lord in Edward the Confessor's reign was called Gamel. We know from the Domesday survey that Gamel also held land at Gomersal and Mirfield to the south of Bradford. We know very little else about him, but most, if not all, of his lands were given to a Norman called Ilbert de Lacy, as a reward for helping William in his successful campaign of conquest. Other manors that were much later to become suburbs of Bradford, or towns and villages within the Bradford Metropolitan District, are likewise described as waste; most of them were also taken over by Ilbert de Lacey.

Ilbert held a considerable amount of land in Yorkshire (and beyond) as a tenant of the king. Under the feudal system he would have been able to derive an income from his various manors in terms of rents and agricultural produce and, in return for being granted his lands, he was expected to be totally loyal to the king and provide money and military levies when required. As the North was still in need of firm control, Ilbert built strongholds throughout his domain, the most important being Pontefract Castle. When the de Lacey line died out in the early fourteenth century the manor of Bradford became part of

Bronze Age Swastika stone, Ilkey Moor. (Sue Naylor)

the Duchy of Lancaster. By then the king had granted permission for a weekly market (1251) and an annual fair (1294) to be held in the town. The first mention of a parish church also dates from this time, and Bradford may have been developing into something of a local centre, although Bingley (1212) had a market granted by the king earlier than Bradford.

It has been estimated that Bradford had a population of about 650 in 1311, twice the number reckoned to be dwelling there at the time of the Conquest. But the population fell back to about 300 by 1379, probably because of a series of disasters, some natural and some man-made, which afflicted the town in the fourteenth century. Yet the poll tax returns for Bingley, just 6 miles from Bradford, show that in this same year there were 130 households, giving an estimated population of about 500, making the town considerably larger than Bradford – or Leeds or Halifax for that matter. Bingley clearly got off lightly in this period of hardship and sudden catastrophes.

Anyone who has seen the film *Braveheart* knows that William Wallace led a revolt of the Scots against English rule at the end of the thirteenth century.

Although Wallace was captured and executed, the impetus of the revolt continued, and Robert the Bruce comprehensively defeated the English at Bannockburn in 1314. What fewer people know is that after Bannockburn the Scots were able to raid the North of England with total impunity for several years; there was no English army to stop them. Ilkley was sacked in 1314, and a Scottish army spent most of the winter of 1318 at Otley, using the town as a base to raid settlements throughout Airedale and Wharfedale. Attracted by its obvious wealth – especially its large flocks of sheep – the Scots attacked Bolton Abbey, forcing the monks to flee to Skipton Castle for safety. In the same year they raided Bradford and damaged the parish church so much that eventually it had to be rebuilt.

To add to people's woes there was a series of poor harvests in the Bradford area, 1316 being a particularly bad year. People reportedly starved and there were rumours of cannibalism. Raids by the Scots became more sporadic after the 1320s, but a new disaster struck in 1349: the Black Death. This outbreak of bubonic plague devastated England and many parts of Europe, and there were two further outbreaks in 1362 and 1369. It has been estimated that one in three of Europe's population may have died from the epidemic, and depopulation meant that in some parts of England there were not enough people to work the land. Of necessity this labour shortage began to be filled by free tenants who worked for themselves, paying cash rents to their landlord rather than giving him their labour. The old feudal system was beginning to disintegrate.

Feudalism declines

A new class of people was emerging in England – a middle-class of free tenant farmers and freeholders, tradesmen, skilled artisans and what might nowadays be called members of the professions. Chaucer's masterpiece *The Canterbury Tales*, written between 1387 and 1389, introduces the reader to a group of pilgrims, the majority of whom are from this new class. Among the usual nuns and monks there are a doctor, a lawyer, a franklin (i.e. a freeholder), a miller, a carpenter, a haberdasher, a dyer and so on. Judging by some of the surnames of local people, there were members of this emerging class in Bradford at this time, usually involved with the manufacture of cloth. Thus, according to the court rolls, there were people called Walker (fuller), Lister (dyer) and Webster (weaver) all to be found living – and presumably working – in Bradford.

Up until this time cloth production in Yorkshire had mainly been carried out in towns further east, such as York and Beverley. It may be that the West Riding townships, especially Halifax and Bradford, began to get involved in the trade because feudalism had become weaker in the West Riding and so tenant farmers were freer to take up cloth manufacturing to supplement their incomes, something they presumably would have been keen to do, given that the farmland they worked was often relatively poor. Also, the streams that flowed into local valleys were by this time being used to provide the power for fulling mills as well as corn mills. The particularly soft water that is a feature of the Bradford area lent itself well to the fulling process, whereby rough woven cloth is soaked in water and pounded to soften it before dyeing. The proximity of Kirkstall and Bolton abbeys, both of which kept large flocks of sheep, meant that there was a ready supply of wool close at hand.

The legend of the boar

In the earlier part of the twentieth century there were two things that Bradford schoolchildren traditionally used to learn about the history of their city. The first was that wool-packs were hung on the parish church tower to ward off cannon balls during the siege of Bradford in the English Civil War. The second was the story of the wild boar without a tongue. According to legend, at some time when John of Gaunt was Duke of Lancaster and thus the overlord of the manor of Bradford (between 1362 and 1399), the townspeople went in fear of a particularly dangerous wild boar, which roamed Cliffe Wood, close to the parish church. A reward was offered to whoever could kill the beast. A certain John Northrop of Manningham (in some versions the man was called John Rushworth) managed to achieve this. He lay in wait by a well or spring that the boar was known to drink from and shot it with his bow and arrow. Unable to carry the boar away, he cut out its tongue as proof that he had killed it. A little later another man came upon the dead body of the boar, cut off its head and carried it away to claim the reward. This man came to the manor court first, but he was unable to explain why the boar's head had no tongue. Soon afterwards Northrop himself arrived with the tongue as proof that it was he who had slain the animal. At this point the details of the legend begin to diverge. In one version the king himself is in Bradford, ready to reward the boar-slayer; in another version it is John of Gaunt who is present. If the story is indeed true (and who

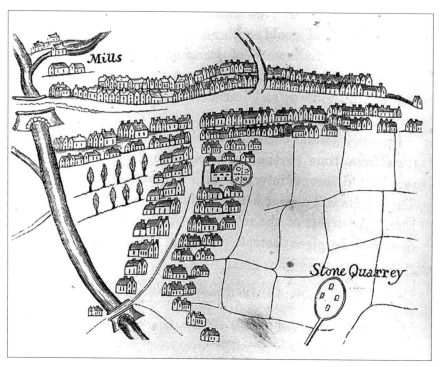

Early map of Bradford. (Courtesy of Bradford Libraries)

is to say that it isn't?) it is more likely that the manorial steward, being the lord of the manor's local representative, was the person in charge of granting the reward. What is certain is that a man called Northrop was given a piece of land in Horton, possibly where Hunt Yard stands today, just off Great Horton Road. This could well have been his reward for killing the wild boar.

One version of the story adds that Northrop (or perhaps Rushworth) was also given the honour of being an attendant of Gaunt, acting as his escort whenever he passed through Bradford on his way to Pontefract Castle. Northrop and his heirs were further obliged to blow three blasts on a hunting horn in Bradford market at Martinmas, the day when rents were due. Apparently this annual horn-blowing custom continued until the nineteenth century. In commemoration of the story, Bradford's original coat of arms featured three hunting horns on a shield, surmounted by a boar's head without a tongue.

It is both interesting and significant that this story of the wild boar is the one that has been passed down to us, for whether folk-tale or hard fact it embodies many of the features that communities everywhere employ to help define themselves. Thus there is a perceived danger to the community and a hero who

bravely tackles the threat; there is a villain who attempts trickery but is caught out by the hero's resourcefulness; and finally there is a reward bestowed on the hero by the community's ruler on behalf of a grateful populace. A story about the Scots destroying the parish church, or one about the horrors of the Black Death, would not be treated as a defining legend in this way, and would of course never be used as a motif on a town's coat of arms. It is even possible that the wild boar legend was created by design in the nineteenth century to give some kind of historical pedigree to a town which, in reality, had little history to speak of prior to the Industrial Revolution.

In contrast to this story of public-spirited courage, which was to become the stuff of local legend, are the records of the manorial court. These itemise not heroic deeds but rather the humdrum petty quarrels and misdemeanours of a population concerned with the daily grind of living year after year in a rather remote part of England. For example, in 1342 John and Alice Renge of Manningham were fined 6*d* for gathering acorns on the lord of the manor's land without his permission. In 1362 Alice Gibwife was fined because her pigs had gone into William Drynker's pastures and had eaten his wheat. In 1359 William Coke was awarded 12*d* in damages because Thomas Walker had taken it upon himself to create a fishpond by damming up Bradford Beck with turf taken from Coke's land.

The later Middle Ages

After John of Gaunt's death in 1399 Bradford was leased out to absentee land-lords, and the Rawson family became stewards of the manor in 1420. They built a manor house in Kirkgate for themselves, dispossessing some local inhabitants in the process. Indeed the Rawsons and their successors, the Bolling family, used their positions quite shamelessly to enrich themselves at the expense of the townspeople. The Bollings blatantly stole cattle and sheep, and on one occasion Raynbron Bolling committed an act of highway robbery, personally assaulting a merchant travelling near Manningham and robbing him of three packs of wool, then demanding a toll of 6*s* 8*d* before allowing him to continue on his way. Complaints about such behaviour generally fell on deaf ears, as justice (such as it was) was normally dispensed by the incumbent steward. But despite suffering under the yoke of these selfish and corrupt landlords, Bradford's cloth-makers were able to make some progress, and the output of woven pieces had increased by the end of the century, helped by the renewal, in 1461, of the charter allowing a market to take place. In 1458 a new parish church was completed.

Between 1452 and 1485 the Houses of York and Lancaster engaged in a civil war to determine who should sit on the throne of England – a conflict known as the Wars of the Roses. It may seem strange to today's citizens to learn that Bradford owed allegiance not to the House of York but to the House of Lancaster. Having said this, the war itself did not directly impinge upon Bradford in the way that the Civil War of the seventeenth century did. The closest that any fighting came to the town was in 1460, when Lancastrian forces attacked the Yorkist garrison at Sandal Castle, near Wakefield. The Duke of York was killed in the fighting. The following year the bloodiest battle ever fought on English soil took place at Towton, near to Tadcaster and about 20 miles from Bradford. Here the Yorkists were victorious. There can be little doubt that men from Bradford would have been obliged to fight for their Lancastrian masters at Towton and that many of them would have died in the conflict, which supposedly resulted in 30,000 deaths. Recent archaeological evidence has shown that a large number of prisoners taken in the battle were later slaughtered (most were clubbed to death), their bodies being thrown into mass graves.

Tudor Bradford

Henry Tudor came to the throne in 1485 and the Tudors ruled England through-out the sixteenth century. Bradford's fortunes, along with the rest of England's, generally took a turn for the better, as a century of destructive dynastic strife gave way to one of relative peace and prosperity. By the end of the sixteenth century England, under Queen Elizabeth, had developed into a self-confident nation. The English were proud of defeating the might of Spain in 1588 and inclined to be rather disdainful – as Shakespeare shows in his fiercely patriotic *Henry V* – of their nearest neighbour across the English Channel. On a local level, John Leland, who visited the area in 1536, was much impressed by what he saw in Bradford: 'A praty quik (lively) market toune ... smaller than Wakefield. It hath one paroche church and a chapel of Saint Sitha. It standith much by cloth-ing and is six miles distant from Halifax and four miles from Kirkstall abbey ... Leeds is as large as Bradeforde, but not so quik.' Generations of Bradfordians have tended to agree with Leland that Bradford is a livelier place than Leeds.

Bradford's parish church stood where the cathedral is nowadays, and most of the town's other buildings were on the opposite side of Bradford Beck, clustered along three thoroughfares, Ivegate, Westgate and Kirkgate, which still remain at the heart of Bradford today. There were bridges across Bradford Beck at the bottom of Ivegate and Kirkgate and the market-place was where the three streets converged. The endings of the street names have nothing to do with gates; they are a version of the Danish word *gata*, the word for street. In southern England, where there was little or no linguistic influence from Scandinavia, Kirkgate would be rendered as Church Street.

There is one piece of evidence that, in addition to a growing cloth trade, Bradford may have been a centre for leather-working and shoe-making. *The Pinner of Wakefield* was a play written in Tudor times, featuring such diverse characters as King Edward IV, the Earl of Leicester and Robin Hood. It contains two interesting references to Bradford: 'I think we are in Bradford, where all the merry shoemakers dwell' and, later in the play, 'This is the town of merry Bradford.'

Whether or not shoe-making was a particular feature of Bradford at this time, there is no doubt that cloth-making was important, as Leland noted. The Dissolution of the Monasteries had an important effect on this, for it meant that the large tracts of land previously owned by great religious houses, such as Kirkstall Abbey, could be parcelled up into smaller holdings and eventually made available for renting or purchase by yeoman farmers, who often combined farming with cloth-making. These men formed an increasingly significant group now that they were becoming more independent of the traditional feudal overlords who had dominated previous generations.

The Dissolution of the Monasteries was an important aspect of the Reformation in England, and by 1559 the country had embraced Protestantism. However, many of the large landowners and powerful families in the North, including the Tempest family of Bradford, remained Catholic throughout this period. One of them, Richard Tempest, had joined the rebellion against King Henry VIII in 1536, which was called the Pilgrimage of Grace. These Catholic rebels objected to the king's anti-papal actions, particularly the destruction of the monasteries, but their revolt was soon quashed. Richard Tempest himself died in prison. Bradford's parish church was taken over by the Protestant Church of England, and almost from the start the incumbent vicars preached a form of Calvinistic Puritanism that seemed to suit the independently minded yeoman farmers and cloth-makers of the area very well.

Signs of growth

Tracing the town's history from the earliest times up to the end of the Tudor period shows us that, in truth, Bradford was a place of only minor significance. But it is possible to see that, especially in the sixteenth century, some features were beginning to develop that would lead to the town eventually achieving much more prominence. The first of these was the growing importance of the domestic textile industry. By the beginning of the seventeenth century Bradford had easily overtaken such places as Ripon and Beverley in terms of cloth output, and this growth trend would continue right up to the time, a couple of centuries later, when the massive impact of the Industrial Revolution changed Bradford for ever.

The second feature was the growth in importance of a new middle-class of yeoman farmers, clothiers and allied tradespeople. Strongly influenced by Puritanism and often at odds with their traditional masters and authority figures, the members of this class would prove fiercely independent and combative in the conflict that was to envelop England in the mid-seventeenth century. Events in the English Civil War would, for a time, place Bradford more centre-stage in the nation's affairs.

two

DISSENTERS AND ANTI-ROYALISTS

B radford's involvement in the English Civil War of 1642 to 1651 was of some importance, particularly in the early years of the conflict. There were certainly some townspeople loyal to the Crown, especially at the outbreak of hostilities, but the majority were always firmly on Parliament's side. There were several reasons for this.

The first concerned the way in which the town was governed. Bradford was a small place – scarcely much more than a village – with a population at the outset of the war estimated to have been no more than 2,500, with perhaps as many again living within the parish of Bradford, which extended a considerable way beyond the town itself. Because much of the agricultural land was too poor to enable families to live by farming alone, many were also involved in cloth production, carried out as a cottage industry. This meant that Bradford was a reasonably busy trading centre in the seventeenth century, but it was not as important in this respect as, for example, Halifax.

There was money to be made in Bradford, however, but those who made it, the members of the merchant and yeoman classes, increasingly resented the way in which the Crown, through its local representatives, sought to deprive them of their wealth. Since the previous century the manor of Bradford had been under the stewardship of the Tempest family of Bolling Hall. The Tempests had always viewed Bradford as their own personal fiefdom, a common enough attitude throughout England at the time, for the whole concept of land tenure and local power was still deeply rooted in medieval feudalism. For many years there had been a growing tension in parts of England, including the West Riding cloth towns, between those charged by the Crown with overseeing the local populace and those individuals who had acquired some wealth through trade, and wanted to have more freedom to run their own lives.

In Bradford's case matters were not helped by the arrogant way in which the Tempests exercised their power. They employed a company of ruffians, dressed

Parish Church under siege, 1642 – engraving. (Courtesy of Bradford Libraries)

in the Tempest livery, who enforced the steward's authority over the towns-people in ways that ranged from the high-handed to the downright brutal. On one occasion complaints were made to the Court of the Star Chamber about four murders, allegedly perpetrated by Tempest's men, which had been hushed up. The Star Chamber was hardly a seventeenth-century version of today's ombudsman – King Charles used it solely to further his own ends and those of his supporters – so nothing was done.

In 1629 Richard Tempest, who was steward at the time, obtained the right to compel all Bradford freeholders to use only his mill to grind their corn. This caused great resentment, which was increased when King Charles, perennially short of money, undertook the kind of asset-stripping that has become quite familiar to us in more recent times. He sold off the manor of Bradford for cash to City of London financiers, and the right to collect the Bradford parish tithes was bought by one of his courtiers, John Maynard. To the yeomen of Bradford, keen to be more independent than in the past, all this smacked of the worst aspects of feudalism. There was also resentment over the Crown's attempts to increase taxes on the export of cloth, especially as the collection of these taxes was frequently farmed out to corrupt favourites of the king. In short the people of Bradford believed that King Charles was misusing his position to tax them unfairly, being responsible for dubious practices that were detrimental to their commercial interests and financially benefiting his London-based courti-ers and favourites.

To cap it all, the king's wife was a Catholic, and so were the Tempests. In fact many people believed that Charles was himself a Catholic in all but name. This leads to yet another reason why Bradford remained firmly within the Parliamentary fold during the forthcoming period of civil strife, namely the town's long-standing tradition of religious dissent and anti-Catholicism. Joseph Lister, who lived in Bradford and kept a journal throughout the Civil War period, expressed the feelings of many of his fellow-townspeople as follows:

> King Charles the First, then upon the throne, to say nothing of his own wicked disposition, did by the constant solicitation of the bloody queen, together with the swarm of Jesuits and evil affected Counsellors, Bishops and men of great estate, place, and trust, all put their heads together to destroy Christ's interest in the nation, and betray their trust every way to the utter ruin and overthrow of Religion, and to cut off the lives of all protestants, and so have enslaved this land to Rome, the mother of harlots whose kingdom is established by blood.

Dissent

Religious dissent flourished in Bradford. The Moravians, possibly feeling that the town would be more tolerant of their non-conformist Hussite views than other places, had opened a church in Little Horton as early as 1638. Many people in Bradford had for years been sympathetic to the teachings of Calvin, mainly because a succession of vicars had, right from the time of Elizabeth I, steadfastly promoted Calvin's Puritan doctrines. The Kempes, father and son, were two such vicars; Christopher Taylor and John Okell were two others. All fell foul of the Church of England's hierarchy from time to time and were upbraided by the archbishop's court in York. The practices the court disapproved of were such things as not wearing a surplice while conducting a service, not making the sign of the cross, and allowing parishioners to receive communion while standing, rather than kneeling.

More serious, in the eyes of the court, were the sermons and lectures that the Puritan vicars delivered as supplements to the prescribed forms of worship. These were known as exercises and had been specifically forbidden by Archbishop Laud in 1633. The ban was ignored in Bradford. The exercises were often delivered on Sunday afternoons in an informal atmosphere and became so popular that the interior of Bradford's parish church had to be extended with galleries to accommodate all those who wanted to come and listen. For people to hear the word of God preached in this way was in marked contrast to the stilted formality of conventional Church of England services, let alone the Latin-based ritual of Catholic worship. These Sunday afternoon exercises reinforced people's adherence to dissenting Puritanism.

Thus, in the secular sphere Bradford's townspeople were increasingly angered by the actions of the king and his local steward, and in the religious sphere dissent from the strictures of the Church's hierarchy had become the norm. And just as the king sought to enforce his rule through the much-despised Tempests, so did the Church of England attempt to enforce its rule by admonishing Bradford's Puritan vicars. In 1639, in a blatant attempt to stifle Puritanism in the town, a new vicar was appointed. This High Church nominee of the Crown was Richard Hudson. There was uproar in Bradford, resulting in a petition that accused Hudson of the following: 'tending to innovation and scandal, all which occasion your petitioner to think he is a man of turbulent spirit, not rightly qualified for such a parish'. The petition fell on deaf ears, and Hudson continued in post, to be succeeded, to the further dismay of the towns-people, by another High Church vicar, Francis Corker.

In 1639 troops were billeted in Bradford to keep the locals, described by Corker as 'very factious and seditious', under tighter control. These troops did not behave any better than Tempest's bullies towards the townspeople, some of whom felt compelled to leave Bradford. Whenever a heavy-handed military presence is imposed upon an unwilling civilian population, the likelihood is that hatred of the occupying force and a desire for retribution will be the most likely outcomes, as was seen in recent times during the troubles in Northern Ireland. To escape from the doctrines and practices espoused by people like Hudson and Corker, which seemed to many to be little more than thinly disguised popery, a number of Bradford's inhabitants even emigrated to New England.

Given what has been described here, it would have been astonishing if the people of Bradford had been anything other than firmly committed to Parliament when the Civil War started in the autumn of 1642.

The Civil War

Most of King Charles's support in the war came from the great landowners and their tenants, both Church of England and Catholic, in the north and west

of England, whereas Parliament's strength lay mainly in the south and east among merchants, smaller land-owners and yeoman farmers, many of whom were Puritans. But there were no exact geographical or social divisions. The Fairfaxes, for example, who quickly became Parliament's leading military commanders in the North, were Yorkshire aristocrats, and although the city of York was firmly in the Royalist camp, the strategically important port of Hull, not too far away, was resolutely Parliamentarian. As neither side had overall control of the North, the aim of both was to

Paper Hall, 1643, in Barkerend Road, close to the then parish church. (Sue Naylor)

consolidate their positions. From the Royalist point of view this meant subdu-ing, by force if necessary, those cloth towns like Bradford that were essentially outposts of the Parliamentarian cause.

As soon as war broke out the occupying soldiers left Bradford to join the main body of the Royalist army, giving the townspeople an opportunity to fortify the town as much as they could, in case the king's forces returned. In late October a force of several hundred Royalists from York did indeed return, having first established a base at Leeds. Although no regular Parliamentarian troops could be called on, the Royalists were beaten off by the townspeople of Bradford, who chased them from the town and even drove them out of nearby Leeds.

The following month the Royalist army in the North had a change of leader-ship, the Earl of Newcastle taking over from the ineffective Earl of Cumberland. Newcastle raised a force of about 9,000 men with which he entered Yorkshire, and he quickly occupied Leeds and Wakefield before turning his attention to Bradford. At the time there were no regular Parliamentarian troops in the town, and many of the able young men had left to join Sir Thomas Fairfax and his father, Lord Fairfax, who together commanded Parliament's army in the North. Consequently Newcastle must have assumed that taking Bradford would be little more than a routine mopping-up operation, so he assigned a comparatively small force of about 800 men under the command of Sir William Saville to see to the task.

The Battle of the Steeple

Saville marched on Bradford from Leeds, and positioned his artillery just a few hundred yards to the north of the town on the high ground close to where Carlton Bolling School now stands. From here the Royalists could direct their fire at the tower of the parish church, which was occupied by the few defenders who had muskets. The rest of the defenders, armed with makeshift weapons, manned the barricades that had been constructed close to the church.

As night approached Saville called on the inhabitants to surrender, but they stubbornly refused. It was clear that the next day Bradford's defending force of about 300 ill-equipped irregulars would have to take on more than double that number of trained and well-equipped soldiers. Joseph Lister, who was about fifteen years old at the time, was one of the defenders. He later recorded his impressions of the next day's fighting as follows: 'We drew up close to the town in order to receive them; they had the advantage of the ground which exposed us more to their cannon from which we sustained some loss but our men defended these passes so well by which they were to descend that they got no ground of us.'

Despite the courage of the defenders it seemed likely that the superior number of Royalists must eventually prevail. But divine providence (or so it was interpreted by the pious Puritans of Bradford) intervened at this point. A sudden blizzard sprung up, blowing directly into the faces of the Royalists, and soon afterwards one of their cannon exploded, killing and wounding several men standing nearby. Saville's soldiers were so disheartened by this turn of events that they retreated to Leeds in some disorder. They were also clearly surprised by the tenaciousness of the defenders, over whom they had expected to score an easy victory. As has been shown often enough, when people are defending their homes their courage and fighting spirit can often compensate for a lack of formal military training and a shortage of weapons. It must also be remembered that the defenders were, in the main, Puritans, passionately convinced that they were doing God's will by combating the corrupt High Church followers and their papist fellow-travellers.

There was no time for complacency. The townspeople of Bradford understood only too well that the Royalists would soon return in force and that they must therefore prepare themselves. All the next day (a Saturday) was given over to strengthening the town's defences, including hanging woolpacks on the parish church tower in order to ward off cannon balls. Joseph Lister described these

preparations as follows: 'We set about fortifying ourselves with the greatest alacrity, resolution and assiduity, in order, if possible, to frustrate every attempt that might be made upon us to deprive us of our liberties and properties.'

The Royalists attacked on the Sunday morning, knowing that their adversaries would be at their prayers. However, this rather underhand tactic was not successful, and the Royalist cavalry was spotted by look-outs and forced to retreat, under fire from the town's defenders. Fire was exchanged between attackers and defenders for the rest of the morning, with neither side being able to gain an advantage. Then, just after midday, a group of so-called clubmen, armed with a variety of improvised weapons, arrived from Bingley, soon to be followed by reinforcements from Halifax. The defenders now had superiority in numbers, and they swarmed out of the town to engage the Royalists in savage hand-to-hand fighting, during which little mercy was shown, as is described in this contemporary account: 'A stout gallant officer, commanding a company of foot came running down a field intending to come into the church. Two of the townsmen met him and struck him down; he cried out for quarter and they, poor men, not knowing the meaning of it said, "Aye, they would quarter him" and so they killed him.' Other Royalists who had surrendered were also killed out of hand and their bodies stripped. Civil wars are notorious for being particularly brutal, especially when the combatants are irregulars or civilians unfamiliar with the established rules and etiquette of warfare. In recent times one need look no further than events in the former Yugoslavia or in Rwanda to see the truth of this.

In Bradford's case, the brutality of 18 December 1642 was to have serious repercussions for the town. The Royalists were unlikely to forget or forgive the atrocities they believed their comrades had suffered and the term 'Bradford Quarter' was coined, an expression with a bitter, ironic meaning. In future it was likely that no mercy at all would be shown to enemies who had surrendered. Soldiers or civilians, male or female, the expectation was that they would be killed.

But all that was still to come. For the moment the Parliamentarians were able to celebrate a victory, which they decided to call the Battle of the Steeple. More importantly, they took the opportunity to use their success for propaganda purposes. Not long after the battle they published a pamphlet in praise of Sir Thomas Fairfax, called *The Rider of the White Horse*. This purported to be 'A true and faithful relation of that famous and wonderful victory at Bradford, obtained by the club-men there, with all the circumstances thereof'.

Bolling Hall. (Sue Naylor)

As the American politician Hiram Johnson once said, 'The first casualty when war comes is truth.' According to the account in *The Rider of the White Horse*, Sir Thomas Fairfax had been the hero of the hour, inspiring and leading the plucky townspeople of Bradford to a resounding triumph over fearful odds. This was a total fabrication. Fairfax was not involved in the battle at all, as he was nowhere near Bradford at the time. Furthermore, while it is true that the Royalists had received a bloody nose from the Bradford irregulars and the Bingley clubmen, the battle was really not much more than a minor engagement. It had only involved a relatively small detachment of Newcastle's army, which continued to control much of the West Riding – including Leeds and Wakefield. But the propaganda value of the Battle of the Steeple, as presented in the pamphlet, was considerable and had the desired effect. It enhanced Sir Thomas Fairfax's reputation as a military commander, and it raised the morale of Parliamentarians throughout England at a time when the Royalists seemed to have the upper hand.

It was not until January 1643, several weeks after the victory he was supposed to have achieved, that Sir Thomas actually entered Bradford with his troops. Straight away he could see that the town was, in his words, 'very untenable', but nevertheless he asked his father's permission to use it as a base to conduct operations against the other Yorkshire towns still in Royalist hands. He reasoned that capturing these would lead to a firmer foothold for the

Parliamentarians in their struggle to control the North. The operations, if successful, would also offer some relief to places whose commerce was suffering greatly. The Royalists had imposed what amounted to a trade embargo in the West Riding; in particular, they forbade merchants from transporting their cloth to Hull for export because the port remained in Parliament's hands. In a letter to his father, Sir Thomas wrote as follows: 'These parts grow very impatient of our delay in beating [the Royalists] out of Wakefield and Leeds, for by them all trade and provision are stopped so that the people of these clothing towns are not able to subsist.'

Permission was granted for action to commence, and Sir Thomas launched an attack against Leeds in late January 1643. This was so successful that his troops also liberated Sherburn and Pontefract from the Royalists and drove Newcastle's troops back as far as Tadcaster, where they were able to regroup. Later in the spring of that year, still using Bradford as his base, Sir Thomas took Wakefield.

Newcastle now realised that if he were to have any chance of regaining control of the West Riding he would have to strike at the Fairfax centre of operations, Bradford. The Royalists also had unfinished business in the town. After their defeat at the Battle of the Steeple they wanted revenge. The Fairfaxes were aware that Bradford could not easily be defended, because of its location in a bowl-shaped valley, surrounded on almost all sides by hills. The town, it is true, had withstood several attacks from the Royalists the previous year, but these had been on a comparatively small scale. This time it was likely that Newcastle would come with the full might of his army. If his troops occupied the hills surrounding Bradford it would be very difficult to withstand them, because they would be able to dominate the town with their artillery. Waiting in the town for the Royalists to attack would certainly be a serious mistake, so even though they knew that their forces would be outnumbered, the Fairfaxes thought the best option was to confront Newcastle's army in open country between Bradford and Wakefield. In his memoirs Sir Thomas wrote: 'We resolved next morning with a party of three thousand men to attempt [Newcastle's] army, as they lay in their quarters three miles off, hoping to put him into some distraction which could not by reason of the unequal number be done in any other way.'

The two armies met at a place that nowadays is close to the small town of Drighlington. That place is Adwalton Moor.

The Battle of Adwalton Moor

Although the number of combatants involved at Adwalton Moor was relatively small, the battle itself was of major significance. If the Fairfaxes had won – which they nearly did – the Royalists would have suffered a serious setback and their power in the North would have all but disappeared. York, their principal base, would most likely have fallen, and their overall strategy to defeat the Parliamentarians would have been in jeopardy.

London, with all its wealth, was in the hands of Parliament. Charles's great desire, therefore, was to capture the capital, but before he could do that he had to ensure that the North was totally secure. If that could be achieved, the plan was that Newcastle's army could then be redeployed to join with other Royalist forces to threaten London, instead of being involved in the seemingly endless cat-and-mouse skirmishing across Yorkshire that had characterised much of the first year of the war in the North. As it turned out, even though the Royalists were victorious at Adwalton Moor they were not able to capitalise on their success, because other factors came into play – as shall be seen later in this chapter.

On the morning of 30 June the Fairfaxes led their army of about 3,000 soldiers, with possibly another 1,000 irregulars, out of Bradford and towards Wakefield. At Adwalton Moor, just a few miles from Bradford, Newcastle had drawn up his army of about 9,000 men on a front of some 700yds, along the main ridge of the moor. The Parliamentarians drew up their force approximately 500yds from the Royalist line. Lord Fairfax was in overall command of the Parliamentarians and his son, Sir Thomas, commanded the troops on the right flank. Of crucial importance was the fact that the undulating terrain of the moor meant that Sir Thomas could not really see what was happening to the rest of the army to his left.

At first things went well for the Fairfaxes. Royalist charges were repulsed and Sir Thomas's musketeers, on the right flank, began to inflict heavy losses on the Royalist cavalry, whose commander, Colonel Howard, was killed early in the battle. However, things swung in the Royalists' favour after a charge by mounted pikemen broke through the Parliamentarians' left flank, causing the troops there to retreat. This was the key moment in the battle. Sir Thomas offered no support to his beleaguered comrades to his left, for the simple reason that he was not aware they were in difficulties. Having lost contact with the rest of the army, he could not appreciate that its left flank and, before long, its centre were about to break. Seizing this advantage, the Royalists launched fresh cavalry charges, and soon the entire Parliamentarian army was leaving the field and fleeing back towards Bradford. Lord Fairfax fled first to Leeds and then to Selby, then to the safety of Parliament's stronghold at Hull.

Sir Thomas fled first to Halifax and then to Bradford, where the remnants of the defeated Fairfax army also sought refuge. About 700 of their number had been killed in the battle. The next day Newcastle's army arrived and completely surrounded Bradford, firing on the parish church and on houses in the town with impunity. Newcastle himself made his headquarters at Bolling Hall, home of the detested Tempests and less than a mile from the town centre. As the next day was a Sunday a ceasefire was declared, though the Royalists took the opportunity to reposition their guns so that they would be more effective when fighting resumed. Under a flag of truce talks took place between the adversaries, but these came to nothing.

Cathedral Tower today. (Sue Naylor)

'Pity Poor Bradford'

The inhabitants of the town feared the worst. Lister described the atmosphere in the town that Sunday night: 'Oh what a night and morning was that in which Bradford was taken! What weeping and wringing of hands! None expected to live any longer than till the enemies came into town, the Earl of Newcastle having charged his men to kill all and to give them all "Bradford quarter".'

Knowing how desperate the situation was, Sir Thomas waited until night-fall, and then broke out with fifty horsemen under cover of darkness, leaving Bradford to its fate. He made for Otley first, hoping to avoid Royalist troops and thence make his way to Hull to join his father. A running fight took place just outside Bradford, resulting in the death of two of Fairfax's officers. There is some evidence that a skirmish may also have taken place at Baildon, about 3 miles from Bradford. Indentations possibly caused by musket balls can still be seen in the walls of Baildon Hall. Sir Thomas's wife also tried to escape Bradford by carriage, but she was captured just outside the town by Newcastle's troops. However, showing commendable chivalry, Newcastle arranged for her to have safe passage to rejoin her husband.

As Lister wrote, the townspeople expected to be massacred the next day, but to their surprise and immense relief this did not happen. A story soon began to circulate that Newcastle had had a change of heart while in bed at Bolling Hall on the Sunday night. It was said that a ghostly figure – a woman – appeared and begged him to 'Pity poor Bradford'. Whether or not he was really visited by a ghost (or even by a more tangible female, pleading Bradford's case), Newcastle certainly showed Bradford unexpected mercy. The remnants of the defeated Parliamentarian army surrendered to him the next day, but only a few people were actually killed as the Royalists moved in to occupy the town. Lister noted the following: 'I think that not more than half a score were slain and that was a wonder, considering what hatred and rage they came against us.' He left Bradford, but returned a few days later to observe the following: 'I found few people left, but most of them scattered and fled away. I lodged in a cellar that night, but oh! What a change was made in the town in three days' time! Nothing was left to eat or drink, or lodge upon, the streets being full of chaff and feathers and meal, the enemies having emptied all of the town of what was worth carrying away and were now sat down and encamped near Bowling [sic] Hall and there kept a fair and sold the things that would sell.'

It is of course quite likely that the story of the ghostly apparition and Newcastle's change of heart was invented by the Royalists themselves as a piece of propaganda. Now that they were firmly in control of Bradford and the other towns of the West Riding – at least for the time being – it would have made sense for Newcastle and his men to appear magnanimous in victory, for this would send a clear message that their military superiority was so great that they could afford to be generous to those they had so decisively crushed. The story of a merciful conqueror might also have been intended to persuade waverers to abandon the Parliamentarian cause, and even change sides.

Newcastle was rewarded by the king by being made a marquis. He had succeeded in securing the North for the Crown, and nearly every town in Yorkshire was now in Royalist hands, the one important exception being Hull, which the

Parliamentarians managed to hang on to. However, Newcastle found that he could not exploit his success and help the king's cause elsewhere in England. He was unable to march his soldiers southwards to threaten London, because the forces of Oliver Cromwell's Eastern Association effectively barred the way. Not sure of his next move, he hesitated throughout the rest of 1643, and this meant that the opportunity to capitalise on the victory at Adwalton Moor was lost. Instead it was the defeated Parliamentarians who were galvanised into positive action by Newcastle's success. In the months following their defeat they concluded an alliance with the Presbyterian Scots. This would lead to the Royalists being totally routed in the North within the next twelve months.

Statue of Cromwell on City Hall façade. (Sue Naylor)

Throughout the autumn of 1643 and into 1644 the growing involvement of the Scots on Parliament's side increased pressure on the Royalist headquarters at York. The Royalists now had to prepare to meet the Scots, as well as trying to contain the Parliamentarians in Hull and prevent them from liaising with the West Riding towns whose populations remained sympathetic to Parliament. This sympathy turned to action in early 1644, and there were skirmishes around Halifax as local Parliamentarians grew in confidence, emboldened by the promise of help from the Scots. In March 1644 the Fairfaxes felt able to make an incursion into West Yorkshire from Cheshire and a detachment of their army, led by Major-General John Lambert, took several towns, including Bradford, from the Royalists. Lambert described his campaign as follows: 'We marched out of Cheshire to Sowerby and from thence to Halifax and back to Keighley and so to Bradford.'

The Royalists attempted to retake Bradford in late March, but were defeated. The following month they were defeated again, this time at Selby, and on 2 July the biggest battle of the Civil War was fought at Marston Moor, near York. The Parliamentarians, under Lord Fairfax and with their Scottish Presbyterian allies, decisively defeated the Royalists, under Newcastle and Prince Rupert. The North was henceforward completely under the control of Parliament. This led eventually to the final defeat of the Royalists and ultimately to the trial and execution of King Charles.

During the course of the two years 1642-44 Bradford had suffered sieges, occupations, battles, privations, destruction and death. Writing in 1878 about the town's involvement in the Civil War, Abraham Holroyd commented on the loss of life: 'It is said that so many people were buried in or near Vicar Lane that it obtained the unenviable designation of "Dead Lane" – so called even now.'

Aftermath of the Civil War

The Civil War continued, with intermissions, for another seven years, but the focus moved away from the North and Bradford was no longer directly involved. There is evidence from the parish register that Bradford's population may have declined at this time, for there were considerably fewer baptisms in 1659 (113) than there had been in 1639 (209), although the existence of separate registers held by the Quakers and other Nonconformist groups makes the town's true birthrate hard to assess. Nonetheless, it has already been noted that there was an exodus from the town in the years immediately before the war because of unpopular vicars and the bad behaviour of the soldiers billeted in Bradford. Lister wrote of people fleeing the town when it was captured by Newcastle in the summer of 1643, and it is likely that some never returned. There was also an outbreak of bubonic plague in the town in 1645, victims being buried in an isolated area of woodland between Bradford and Shipley. All these events would probably have reduced Bradford's population and thus, for a time, its influence.

Despite the town's unwavering loyalty to the Parliamentarian cause during the Civil War, no special favours or rewards were forthcoming from Oliver Cromwell's regime during the years of the Protectorate (1653-60) and, unlike Leeds and Halifax, Bradford was not given a Member of Parliament. It was only in the last part of the century that Bradford began to regain its commercial momentum, with a new emphasis on the production of worsted cloth.

The Protectorate was not popular. Many of those who had fought against the Crown in the Civil War welcomed the restoration of the monarchy in 1660. It is said, for example, that Sir Thomas Fairfax, one of Parliament's outstanding generals, lent his horse to Charles II when he arrived to claim his throne. But in the cloth towns of the West Riding some hostility towards the Crown remained,

Adwalton Moor battlefield. (Sue Naylor)

as shown by the Farnley Wood Plot of 1663. A group mainly from Leeds, but with some support from over a dozen prominent Bradfordians, hatched a plot to overthrow the restored monarchy – motivated by a fear that Charles II intended to re-establish Catholicism in England, and that non-Catholics, especially Nonconformists, would therefore be persecuted. The plot was a total failure, and most of the conspirators were quickly rounded up and executed for treason in York and Leeds, although most of the Bradford men seem to have escaped capture and may have fled abroad.

In fact, despite Charles's sympathy for Catholicism and James II's attempts to make England a Catholic country once more, Nonconformity continued to grow as the century progressed, particularly in those towns (like Bradford) that had a strong tradition of Puritanism and had supported Parliament during the Civil War. George Fox, the founder of the Society of Friends, had visited Bradford in 1652, during the time of the Protectorate, and from about this time Quakers and other Nonconformists in the town were given – quite unusually – permission to keep their own registers of births, marriages and deaths alongside the official parish records. There is evidence that a Baptist group was active in

Bradford in 1655. In 1662 Jonas Waterhouse, keeping up the local tradition of being at odds with the Church of England hierarchy, was expelled from his living as Vicar of Bradford for refusing to accept High Church doctrines. He continued to preach in Bradford as an independent. And in the Leeds Quarter Session Rolls of 1689 the following entry shows that a group of dissenters met for worship in what is now Lidget Green, about 2 miles from Bradford: 'An assembly of Dissenting Protestants in and about Bradford do make choice of the house of Richard Whitehouse, clerk, of Lidgate [sic] near Clayton.' Further evidence of the strength of dissent in Bradford is provided by the court records at York. Between 1665 and 1671 more than thirty people from the parish of Bradford were prosecuted because they had neglected to attend divine service at the parish church, which was, after the expulsion of Jonas Waterhouse, once again under the control of a High Church vicar.

While the tide of dissent suffered setbacks, especially when James II was on the throne (1685-88), the prevailing undercurrent from the Civil War onwards was slowly moving towards more tolerance. The accession of William and Mary in 1688 and the Toleration Act of the following year confirmed this, and doubt-less made life easier for Nonconformists. In Bradford a chapel for dissenters was opened in Little Horton in 1688 and a Baptist chapel was founded in Heaton in 1689. In 1698 a Friends' Meeting House opened on the Wakefield road.

By contrast the Church of England failed to flourish in Bradford. It was only in the nineteenth century that a second Anglican church was built. By that time a new wave of religious Nonconformity – Methodism – had arrived in the town, and that was to have a significant impact. But a greater impact, as the eight-eenth century unfolded, was provided by Bradford's incipient transformation into a major manufacturing centre, based on the production of worsted cloth.

three

A PRELUDE TO GREAT THINGS

Bradford in the Eighteenth Century

At the start of the eighteenth century Bradford was still an insignificant place, but by the end of the century it was ready to embark upon a period of unparalleled expansion. What were the conditions that allowed this small town to move rapidly from rural backwater to industrial powerhouse, gaining an international reputation? What were the seeds planted in the eighteenth century (and even before) that were to come to such an astonishing fruition just a few decades later?

Local industry

It has been estimated that fewer than 4,000 people lived in Bradford in 1700 and, although the town had by that time largely recovered from the Civil War, it was still impoverished, as was much of the West Riding. Daniel Defoe, the author of *Robinson Crusoe*, made a comprehensive journey through the country in the 1720s and subsequently recorded his observations in *A Tour Through the Whole Island of Great Britain*. In his book he speaks of the poverty of Yorkshire people, who 'scarcely sowed enough corn to feed their poultry'.

As noted in earlier chapters, it was the very fact that much of the agricultural land in the Bradford area was of an inferior quality which led farmers to take up cloth-making in order to make some kind of a living. Cloth production before 1778 (when the first textile mill was built) was, therefore, a cottage industry that involved all members of the family; if not engaged in farming, they spent their days turning raw wool into woven cloth. Visitors to Haworth can still see, in the main street of the town, good examples of the cottages where this work went on, although nowadays many of the premises have become cafés and gift shops.

Crucial to this cottage industry was the wool stapler. He was the merchant who travelled widely to purchase raw wool and distribute it to the domestic manufacturers, who then produced woven pieces to sell in the market-place. In 1773 a piece hall was built in Bradford for this trade. It no longer exists, although Piece Hall Yard is still there, nowadays part of a traffic-free zone in the centre of the city. The Halifax Piece Hall, built in 1779 with over 300 rooms for buying and selling textile pieces, still exists, though its main function today is to house bric-a-brac shops and the like, catering for tourists. The staplers were what might be termed the lubricating oil of the wool and worsted trade. They constituted a group, along with the local mine owners, which by the second half of the century was providing the necessary energy – and capital – for the future development of Bradford.

By the eighteenth century it was the production of worsted cloth rather than woollen cloth that was beginning to predominate, especially in the communities, such as Thornton and Haworth, in the west of the Bradford area; woollen cloth was still for a time the main product further east, in places like Bowling and Wibsey. This east-west division was further refined until in the next century Leeds became the centre of Britain's woollen cloth industry and Bradford became Britain's 'Worstedopolis', producing worsted cloth for suits and fashionable clothing. Readers seeking detailed knowledge about the various processes involved in textile production should look elsewhere, but in simple terms the difference between woollen cloth and worsted cloth is that the latter requires the long fibres of wool to be combed so that they all lie in the same direction. A finer yarn can then be spun, which is woven to produce a smooth fabric. Wool combing, therefore, was an important process. Traditionally done by hand and later by machines, it was a key factor in Bradford's development as the major centre of the worsted industry in Britain. The patron saint of the woollen industry is St Blaise, an early Christian bishop from Armenia who, according to legend, was martyred by being stabbed to death with iron wool combs. A statue of Blaise, wool comb in hand, adorns the front of the Wool Exchange in the heart of the city.

Although the soil might not have been the most productive for farming, there was an abundance of stone in the locality, easily quarried and suitable for building. Visitors to Bradford, even today, often remark on the preponderance of stone rather than brick buildings, and it moved J.B. Priestley in *English Journey* (1934) to remark on 'the authentic, queer, carved out of the Pennines look of Bradford and some of the other [nearby] towns'. Most of the local stone is millstone grit, a hard sandstone of great strength which is so weather-proof and durable that it has been exported for use in the con-

struction of underwater docks. Stone like this was needed when the great mills and warehouses were built in Bradford and throughout the West Riding in the nineteenth century. Floors needed to be strong enough to carry heavy machinery, and slabs of millstone grit were ideal for this. Its abundance and the fact that it could be worked easily into building blocks also meant that low-cost dwellings could be quickly thrown up when the time came to house thousands of mill-workers, once the Industrial Revolution had really begun to take off.

As was noted in Chapter One, iron was found and worked in Bierley as early as Celtic times, but it was not until the late eighteenth century that important ironworks were established, mainly in the south of Bradford and notably at Low Moor and Bowling. By this time coal rather than charcoal was being used for smelting. It could be found throughout the Bradford area, as the town lay right at the north-western edge of the great Yorkshire coalfield. There is evidence that primitive coal mines had existed throughout the area from the middle-ages and by the eighteenth century Bradford's coal-mining industry was growing in importance. Supplies of iron and coal near at hand would obviously be very important in the nineteenth century when the time came to build and power the machinery of the new industrial age.

So, stone was available for building, coal and iron were available for making machines and enabling them to run, a long tradition of cloth-making was present, and the local soft water was ideal for various processes in cloth production. But these factors do not fully explain what happened next. The town's location was not ideal: Bradford was in a Pennine valley and not easily accessible. Several regions of England, notably East Anglia and the West Country, had long traditions of cloth manufacturing; other places also had access to coal and iron ore. So why did Bradford succeed? One factor is clear. While Bradford (one presumes) did not have a monopoly of energetic risk-takers, intent on making their fortunes, there were certain individuals in the eighteenth and nineteenth centuries who, as we shall see, were vitally important in Bradford's successful development. And there was one more piece of the jigsaw – communication.

Improved communications

Historians have traditionally subscribed to the view that what really defined the Industrial Revolution was the greater interaction of communities; improved communication was all-important. At the start of the eighteenth century the roads throughout most of England were in a very poor state, no better really than they had been in medieval times. A statute of 1555 required each parish to maintain the roads in its locality, but this obligation was often ignored. There were stories of horses drowning in rain-filled potholes on the Great North Road. It took at least nine hours to travel by road from Bradford to York and four or five days to travel from Bradford to London. Making use of waterways could make life easier, and those Yorkshire towns (such as Leeds and Selby) that had access to navigable waterways had an advantage over a place like Bradford, where traders had to rely largely on packhorses traversing rough tracks for the movement of their merchandise.

Naturally the people who were most frustrated by the lack of adequate roads were the merchants and manufacturers. This class was now beginning to grow in Bradford, as cloth production and coal mining increased, and its members were at the forefront of moves to improve the roads. Improvements eventually came via the creation of turnpike trusts, private sector initiatives whereby local businessmen and landowners obtained, through Act of Parliament, permission to charge tolls on a stretch of road. A proportion of the money thus gained was then reinvested in the maintenance and improvement of the highway. From a merchant's point of view the turnpikes were a resounding success, for they improved communications considerably and so benefited trade. Bradford was first linked to the network of turnpikes in 1734, from which time it lay on a main road between Leeds and Manchester. Six years later a second major turnpike between Selby and Halifax was routed through Bradford. Local businessmen such as John Hustler – of whom more later – were subscribers to the trusts, and so was Jeremiah Rawson, who was then Bradford's lord of the manor.

By the middle of the century, therefore, Bradford was much better linked not only to other growing centres of trade and industry in Yorkshire, such as Wakefield and Leeds, but also to places further afield, including London. By the end of the century a daily stagecoach to London was well established. The turnpikes were also important for enabling a more effective mail service to develop, very necessary if trade was to flourish.

However, there was a downside to the turnpikes as far as some people were concerned. The nineteenth-century Bradford historian John James commented: 'The turnpikes were, by the lower class, universally regarded as an obnoxious regulation, more adopted for the convenience of the wealthy por-

Handloom weavers cottages in Little Horton. (Sue Naylor)

tion of the community, whose carriages could hardly pass on the old roads, than the benefit of such a [lower] class.' Everyone using the turnpikes, whether rich or poor, had to pay a toll, so naturally there was resentment among people who even at the best of times existed in poverty. And of course there were some people, as in any age, who were simply suspicious and even fearful of change. In 1753 there was a major outbreak of anti-turnpike rioting in Bradford, involving hundreds of people who burned down the toll-houses at Tyersal and Wibsey, as well as destroying the toll bars at Apperley Bridge and Bradford Moor. Abraham Balme, a Bradford cloth manufacturer and a leading subscriber to the local turnpike trust, had his house attacked by an angry mob. But outrages such as these could not stand in the way of progress; the turnpikes were there to stay – although before very long they gave way to more effective modes of transport, first canals and later railways. What was probably the last of the turnpike trusts in the Bradford area, the Bradford to Colne Trust, was eventually wound up in 1878, having outlived its usefulness by many years.

The coming of the canals

The next stage of Bradford's development was the building of a canal, and this, possibly more than anything else, was the real catalyst for the town's phenomenal expansion. While the turnpikes had certainly been an improvement over the old packhorse routes, a canal enabled far larger and heavier quantities of goods to be transported at a more economic cost than could ever be managed by road. It is interesting to note that the men who had the vision and the drive to achieve the construction of the Bradford Canal, and link it to a waterway system that would eventually connect the North Sea with the Irish Sea, were not initially concerned so much with shifting woollen and worsted products as they were in moving coal and stone.

In 1764 the *York Courant* carried the following announcement: 'As the Rivers Aire and Ribble may be so easily joined at different places and rendered navigable between Leeds and Preston, at an expense which gentlemen who have estates on the banks may readily supply, it is thought proper to mention [this] to the public at this juncture.'

Inspired by the success of the Bridgewater Canal, which had opened in 1760, a group of Bradford businessmen met at the Sun Inn in 1766. Leeds was already linked by the Aire and Calder Navigation to the River Ouse and thence to the Humber and the port of Hull. The grand design, therefore, was for a new canal that would start at Leeds, have a link to Bradford, and then follow Airedale northwestwards, crossing the Pennines via the Aire Gap to enter Lancashire, eventually terminating at the port of Liverpool. In the short term the Bradford entrepreneurs who raised the bulk of local capital (the rest coming from the City of London) were interested in creating a waterway that would enable Bradford's coal to be transported to the Skipton area, where it would be traded for Craven limestone, which would then be used in Bradford's ironworks and as a building material.

But in the longer term these Bradford men were intent on having overall control of the whole length of the canal, right from Leeds to Liverpool, including taking a share of the profits from the Lancashire collieries near which the canal would be routed. John Stanhope, a lawyer and Bradford landowner, with interests in mining and cloth, put up £4,000 for the scheme. When Stanhope died in 1770 John Hustler became the main driving force behind the project, and he gained Parliament's permission to commence the work, with James Brindley appointed as chief engineer. When Brindley died in 1772 John Longbotham, formerly the project's clerk of works, took over this key role.

The Five Rise Locks, Bingley. (Sue Naylor)

Work began in 1770, but the entire length of the canal from Leeds to Liverpool – 127 miles – was not completed until 1816 and at a cost of £1.2 million, rather more than Brindley's original estimate of £260,000. A link to Manchester via the Bridgewater Canal was opened in 1820. However, some stretches of the canal were in operation much earlier. On the Yorkshire side of the Pennines the stretch from Shipley to Skipton was completed by 1774, and by 1777 the canal ran all the way from Leeds to Gargrave.

The stretch beyond Shipley required quite remarkable feats of engineering to be carried out at Bingley. Longbotham designed and built two flights of locks here, Five Rise Locks and Three Rise Locks. (Technically these two flights are really staircases, with the top gate of one pound acting as the bottom gate of the pound above, and so on.) Five Rise Locks is the steepest flight of locks in the United Kingdom, with a rise of about 59ft over a distance of 320ft, giving a gradient of about one in five. The smaller Three Rise Locks, which is just a couple of hundred yards away, has a rise of about 30ft. Both flights were opened in March 1774, and a crowd estimated at 30,000 was in attendance to

Plaque commemorating John Nelson's imprisonment (friend of Wesley) in Ivegate dungeon. (Courtesy of Bradford Libraries)

watch the first barge make the descent of Five Rise. The locks, which are the most spectacular feature of the Leeds and Liverpool Canal, have attracted visitors ever since.

The Bradford Canal

In the same year that the Bingley locks were completed a 3 mile branch canal with ten locks was opened, linking the centre of Bradford to the main canal at Shipley. This was a defining moment. The town was now connected to a waterway system that was to provide low-cost access to the industrial regions of Yorkshire, Lancashire and beyond, including the ports of Hull and, eventually, Liverpool. Bradford was now on the map, and the days of laboriously transporting goods by carts along expensive turnpikes, or by packhorse over steep moorland tracks, were numbered. From now on Bradford manufacturers had a facility that would enable them to trade coal, stone and iron with many parts of England, and worsted cloth with the world at large.

The cost of this short but immensely important stretch of canal was £6,000, and Hustler was again one of a group of Bradford entrepreneurs that raised the necessary capital. Alongside his many other commercial activities, Hustler was the treasurer, until his death in 1790, of the company that controlled

the entire length of the Leeds and Liverpool Canal. The headquarters of the company was in Bradford until 1850. By that time the Bradford Canal had become a public health hazard (dealt with more fully in the next chapter), and its commercial viability was also suffering from increasing competition from the railway; Bradford was connected to the rail network in 1846.

The Bradford Canal eventually closed in 1922, and the waterway was filled in. Traces of its route can still be seen alongside the busy Canal Road, which runs between Bradford and Shipley, and the remains of the actual junction with the Leeds and Liverpool Canal, near Dock Lane in Shipley, are plain to see. The Leeds and Liverpool Canal itself remained open for commercial use until the 1980s, and by the late twentieth century it had become an important rec-reational facility in Airedale and beyond.

Nonconformist men of vision

The opening of Bradford's canal may well have been the defining event that was to launch the town towards industrial fame and fortune, but it was not an Act of God. Nothing would have happened without the vision and energy of certain men living and working in Bradford at the time. Like many who were to succeed them as Bradford's commercial and political leaders in the nineteenth century, most of these men were in the well-established Bradford tradition of Nonconformity. Prominent among them was John Hustler (1715–90), who has already been mentioned. Hustler was one of a small group of Quaker business-men, and besides being a leading investor in local turnpike trusts and the Leeds and Liverpool Canal, he was also instrumental in the building of the Piece Hall in 1773. He also chaired the Worsted Committee, which was set up to regulate aspects of the worsted trade and the export of woollen goods. The Piece Hall boosted Bradford as a centre for the marketing and trading of woollen and worsted textiles. It was also used as a courthouse, and from time to time as a concert hall, before other buildings were constructed specifically to fulfil these functions. Hustler is commemorated by Hustlergate, a city-centre street very close to the site of the Piece Hall that he helped to create.

Edmund Peckover (1757-1818) was another Quaker, born in Norfolk but working as a wool stapler in Bradford from the 1780s. In partnership with Hustler's son (also called John) and Charles Harris, yet another Quaker, Peckover, established the first official Bradford Bank in 1803, although a bank of a kind, also founded by local Quakers, had existed from 1760. Peckover Street in the Little Germany area of central Bradford commemorates this man, who was responsible for enabling capital to be provided for Bradford's expanding industries. Clearly these men lived up to the popular saying that Quakers 'when not in the Meeting House are in the Counting House'. Indeed it seems true that the members of Bradford's various Nonconformist sects, with their independence of mind, their Puritan adherence to thrift and to the Protestant work ethic, were just what the town required to further its commercial progress.

The Quakers were involved in philanthropy too, initiating moves aimed at redressing social injustice. Thus Benjamin Bartlett, William Wilson and William Laud, all eminent Bradford businessmen, joined with Hustler to campaign for the abolition of the slave trade and for the establishment of Sunday schools. This group was also responsible for the founding, in 1774, of Bradford's first literary society and a subscription library, although the initial membership fee of 1 guinea and an annual subscription of 5s. would have effectively debarred most people in Bradford from enjoying the benefits of the library.

Methodism

Methodism quickly took a strong hold in Bradford, the first Wesleyan Society being founded as early as 1747 by John Nelson, whose brand of preaching had earlier outraged the Vicar of Birstall (Nelson's home town) to such an extent that he had contrived to have the itinerant preacher imprisoned and press-ganged into the army. Undeterred, Nelson managed to obtain his release and carried on preaching. John Wesley himself visited Bradford on many occasions, the first time being in 1744, when he preached in Little Horton. He also preached at a hall in the centre of Bradford called the Cockpit, which was located near to where Centenary Square is today. This building was a hotbed of vice, gambling and drinking before being taken over by the Methodists in 1756. The Cockpit had the benefit of an open area to its front, which enabled people to hear Wesley and the other Methodist preachers even when the building was full. Wesley and his associates always drew large crowds wherever they preached.

Much of the appeal of Methodism to the people of Bradford was rooted in the town's long-standing tradition of Puritanism. Wesley himself always remained a

Eastbrook Hall, the 'Methodist cathedral of the North'. (Courtesy of Bradford Libraries)

member of the Church of England, but he favoured a simpler, more accessible form of worship, devoid of what he considered to be the excessive formality and ritual associated with the High Anglican Church. William Grimshaw, the curate of Haworth Parish Church and an associate of Wesley, was responsible for a significant upsurge of Methodism, especially among the poorer classes of Haworth, something that is alluded to in Emily Brontë's *Wuthering Heights*. Wesley and Grimshaw were brilliant evangelical preachers, with the ability to appeal directly to people's emotions. In an age when there was no such thing as mass-media and literacy was still a prerogative of a minority, large-scale public meetings for political or religious purpose, often held outdoors and with an emphasis on skilful oratory, were much more important than today, although preachers such as Billy Graham and Ian Paisley have maintained the tradition into the modern era.

The Methodists were probably the most numerous Nonconformist group in Bradford by the end of the eighteenth century, though the Baptists also had a significant presence. Although the Quakers were a small group they had an influence disproportionate to their numbers, as would also be the case when the German community settled in Bradford in the 1840s (see Chapter Five). The Congregationalists, a group that would come more to the fore in the town's commercial and political life in the nineteenth century, opened their first church in Idle in 1717, while the Presbyterians and the Unitarians also built places of worship, the latter group having their chapel in the centre of the town, near to where City Hall now stands.

The Vestry

Despite many people's adherence to Nonconformity, the Church of England still exercised its power in Bradford. In the absence of any kind of town council, it was largely under the auspices of the parish church and a group of self-appointed leading townspeople that Bradford was administered, though not very effectively according to Cudworth, who observes this in his *Historical Notes on the Bradford Corporation*, published in 1881:

> In dealing with the period embraced in the century preceding the election of the Commissioners in 1803, we are almost by the force of circumstances obliged to notice matters not strictly appertaining to the management of the highways, if indeed the term 'management' be not a misnomer, where so little was attempted by the town's authorities, and everybody did pretty much as they pleased. The Vestry was the ruling authority, and was chary of spending money, being generally disposed towards the principle which has, since its day, been regarded as 'economy,' namely expending as little as possible upon whatever object.

What matters did the Vestry concern itself with? A few examples will suffice. In 1714 it passed a resolution that attempted to suppress street begging. About the same time it tried to regulate the distribution of loaves of oat bread to the poor. Paupers could only collect their loaves once a fortnight if they attended the Sunday morning service at the parish church – rather unfair if they were Nonconformists. Under the auspices of the Vestry the Overseers of the Poor were required to go about the town every three months to ensure that no vagrants had become permanent residents. Householders were forbidden from sub-letting their premises to any incomers without the Vestry's permission. In

Bradford Canal, Bolton Lane Bridge, in 1914. (Courtesy of Bradford Libraries)

1795 the Vestry attempted to curb the problem of pigs being allowed to run at large in the streets. Cudworth is of the opinion that few, if any, of the regulations promulgated by the Vestry had much effect at all. By 1800 the time was ripe for a move towards a different form of local government.

Population growth

Over the course of the eighteenth century Bradford's population substantially increased, with most of the increase coming in the final two or three decades before 1800. Taking the township of Bradford with the neighbouring communities of Bowling, Horton and Manningham, there were an estimated 8,700 inhabitants in 1780, and 13,364 were recorded in the 1801 census. To what extent this quite sudden increase was caused by inward migration, as people moved to the area to seek work, or whether it was the result of a rise in the birth-rate, nobody can be sure. Probably it was a combination of the two, though there is a theory that because the traditional system of apprenticeship was under-developed in the Bradford area, early marriages may have led to an increase in the birth-rate. Children were no doubt seen as a valuable source of labour and family income.

As we know, the population of Britain as a whole was increasing in the second half of the eighteenth century, perhaps because the periodic epidemics of bubonic plague that had ravaged Europe between the fourteenth and the seventeenth centuries had not returned. Outbreaks of diseases such as smallpox, cholera and influenza did of course still occur, but they tended to be more localised, and were possibly less deadly than the earlier plague epidemics that had rapidly spread right across Europe and sometimes wiped out whole communities. Bradford would have its epidemics in the next century, notably a cholera outbreak in the late 1840s, caused by overcrowding and unsanitary living conditions. The town expanded so quickly and in such an unregulated way that for a time, as we shall see in the next chapter, it would almost seem to be out of control.

four

INDUSTRIALISATION AND EXPANSION

And did the Countenance Divine
Shine forth among our clouded hills?
And was Jerusalem builded here
Among these dark Satanic Mills?
William Blake (1757–1827)

The popular belief is that the last line of this verse refers to the grimness of the mills and factories that began to proliferate, especially in the North of England, in the early years of the nineteenth century. A less well-known interpretation is that 'dark Satanic Mills' is actually a reference to churches. Blake was vehemently anti-clerical and firmly believed that organised religion enslaved people. Certainly the lines suggest that rapid and unregulated industrialisation created a hell on earth for the people who had to work in the mills, but there might also be a hint that some manufacturers were not averse to using the clergy, as well as the mill overseer, to keep their employees under tight control.

Slavery

It was not until 1833 that slavery was officially abolished throughout the British Empire, thanks largely to the efforts of William Wilberforce. In practice this meant granting liberty to the thousands of people of African descent who worked on the plantations in the West Indies; there were no slaves as such in Britain by this time. However, there were some who felt that the conditions under which men, women and especially children were compelled to work in the mills of a town like Bradford amounted to slavery in all but name. In 1830 Richard Oastler published a famous letter in the *Leeds Mercury* after being

Darley Street with Christchurch and market stalls, early nineteenth-century engraving. (Courtesy of Bradford Libraries)

approached by John Wood, one of only a handful of Bradford mill owners who appear to have cared much for the welfare of their employees. This is an extract from Oastler's letter:

[There exists] a state of slavery more horrid than the hellish system, colonial slavery. The very streets which receive the droppings of an Anti-Slavery Society are every morning wet by the tears of innocent victims at the accursed shrine of avarice, who are compelled not by the cart whip of the negro slave driver, but by the dread of the equally appalling thong or strap of the overlooker to hasten, half-dressed but not half-fed, to those magazines of British infantile slavery, the worsted mills in the town and neighbourhood of Bradford. Thousands of little children, both male and female, but principally female, from seven to fourteen years of age, are daily compelled to labour from six in the morning to seven in the evening ... with only thirty minutes allowed for eating and recreation.

Oastler's efforts eventually led to the Factory Act of 1847, which limited the hours that women and children were permitted to work, although it was not until 1861 that the provisions of the Act were extended to all workplaces. Oastler was a radical insomuch as he favoured factory reform, yet as a Tory he opposed

the extension of the franchise to the men whose working conditions (and those of their wives and children) he sought to improve. Like Feargus O'Connor, the leader of the Chartists, Oastler was swimming against the tide by wanting a return to a pre-industrial age when – supposedly – everyone knew their place, working families were nourished by a plentiful supply of wholesome food and the pace of work could be determined by the individual, rather than by the demands of steam-powered machinery and the mill overseer. The concept of a Golden Age, when everything (including the weather) was much more pleasant, is a common enough characteristic of society in all eras, including our own, and Oastler can be accused of hankering after some kind of mythical ideal. It cannot be denied, however, that his efforts succeeded in pricking the conscience of some industrialists and MPs, resulting in an amelioration of factory conditions for many children. His bronze statue stands in Northgate, Bradford, depicting him with two small factory children. It was unveiled in 1869 by the Earl of Shaftesbury, the century's foremost advocate of better working conditions for children.

The majority of the mill owners in Bradford were not Tories, like Oastler, but Liberals. These men were often radical enough to favour an extension (albeit limited) of the franchise, but they were generally opposed to government interference in how their manufacturing operations should be conducted. So Oastler's letter and his campaigning aroused some heated opposition, especially among those manufacturers whose sole interest was maximising profits without regard to the human cost of child labour. Some even expressed the

view that a thirteen-hour working day was actually beneficial, as the children were under the constant supervision of adults instead of running wild in the streets – and they were also learning useful workplace skills. Dr Thomas Wilson of Bingley had already stated his opinion in evidence to a committee of the House of Lords in 1818 that a young person's health would not suffer if he or she worked seven days a week, and that there was really no need for any recreation or amusement during the day.

The harsh reality of child labour in Bradford's mills can be deduced from this evidence given by a ten-year-old girl to a Factory Inquiry Commission in the early 1830s: 'I come at six in

Statue of Richard Oastler. (Sue Naylor)

the morning. I go at seven [at night]. The overlooker brays [hits] us if we do not mind our work, with his hands over the head. He does it very often ...' Attitudes to child labour and physical punishment were of course quite different in the early nineteenth century compared with today. At that time it was accepted as perfectly normal that children in farming communities or in cottage industries would do their share of work as soon as they were able, and most parents would have agreed with the adage that sparing the rod spoiled the child. But when people worked on the land, and spinning and weaving were carried out as cottage industries, a certain amount of flexibility was possible. For example, the tradition of Saint Monday could be followed, whereby work could be postponed until another day if so desired and an additional day of rest taken. There was no room for such a tradition in the new steam-powered mills, where often a rigid discipline akin to that of the hated workhouse was used to compel the workers to do what the mill owners required. Later in the century some well-known Bradford manufacturers would further reinforce workplace discipline by demanding that their employees keep to the straight and narrow even when not at work. Workers were expected to attend chapel and abstain from alcohol and if they did not comply they could expect to lose their jobs.

A steam-powered revolution

At the beginning of the century only one steam-powered spinning mill existed in Bradford, that of Robert Ramsbotham, built near Randall Well Street close to where Bradford College now stands. Other spinning mills soon followed, and after the failure of the 1825 strike (see Chapter Eight) weaving too was increasingly carried on in purpose-built mills rather than as a cottage industry. One set of statistics shows that in 1841 there were thirty-eight worsted mills in Bradford, another thirty in nearby Horton, Bowling and Manningham and forty-five in the other smaller communities throughout the wider Bradford area, including no fewer than nineteen in Haworth. A dyeing industry was also established in Bradford in the 1820s, and within ten years this had grown into a major component of the town's textile trade, especially after the Ripleys, father George and son Edward, extended their dyeworks in Bowling and developed the new technique of black dyeing.

Bradford's worsted manufacturers were not slow to innovate. By the 1830s many were combining woollen yarn with a cotton warp to produce a lighter

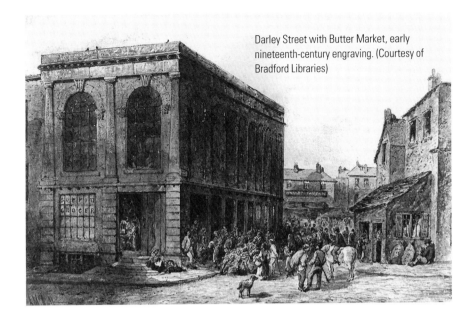

Darley Street with Butter Market, early nineteenth-century engraving. (Courtesy of Bradford Libraries)

cloth, more suited to the current fashion. Because cotton was less expensive than wool, Bradford's worsted cloth could be sold at a lower price than that produced in East Anglia and the West Country. Bradford thus became the undisputed centre of the British worsted trade. Growth accelerated, led by the demand for reasonably priced textile goods in the export market. Even in the late eighteenth century 80 per cent of worsteds produced in the Bradford area had been sold abroad, and half of all woollen goods produced in Yorkshire as a whole were exported to the USA. The overseas market expanded as the nine-teenth century progressed, and by the 1820s the practice of selling in bulk with a rapid turnover had earned the sobriquet 'the Bradford Principle'.

Further evidence of the town's growing importance as a commercial centre lies in the number of stagecoaches with which it was served. In 1814 there were four coaches operating; by 1825 there were twenty-eight. A visitor to Bradford in the 1820s described his impressions of the buoyancy of Bradford's industry as follows:

Worsted stuffs form the staple manufacture of this town and neighbourhood, but broad and narrow cloths, wool-cards and combs are also made here to a con-siderable extent, and the cotton trade from Lancashire has found its way into this district. The spinning of worsted yarn is also a considerable trade here, and has tended not only to enrich individuals, but to promote the general prosperity of the place. No manufacturing town in England has perhaps suffered so little from the depression of trade as Bradford. In war and in peace it has been alike prosperous. It has indeed felt the vicissitudes of trade in common with other places, but the depression has generally been of short duration, and it has been among the first to feel the vivifying effects of the return of prosperous times.

With the construction of so many mills, often surrounded by rows of hastily built back-to-back houses to accommodate the workforce, the landscape of Bradford was being profoundly changed. So were the lives of Bradford's inhabitants, many of whom were witnessing at first-hand the rapid transformation of their birthplace from a semi-rural market town to a totally new kind of industrialised urban milieu, with large numbers of people constantly arriving from other parts of Britain to seek work – all this within the space of one generation. A revolution was taking place in Bradford and, as with all revolutions, it was accompanied by outbreaks of serious unrest and violence.

Unrest

The handloom weavers were at the forefront of reactions to the new world of mills and machinery. In 1822 power looms intended for Warbrick's Mill in Shipley were seized and destroyed by rioters. In 1826 a mob numbering 250 attacked Horsfall's Mill in the centre of Bradford, close to the parish church. The Riot Act was read and troops had to be called to try and disperse the crowd. The crowd did not disperse, and in the fighting that ensued two people were killed and others were wounded.

Other disturbances followed. In November 1837 there were riots in the middle of Bradford when the Guardians of the Poor met at the Court House to put into operation the Poor Law Amendment Act of 1834. This required parishes to group together to set up workhouses; no other means of poor relief were to be offered. Workhouses had existed throughout England from at least the seventeenth century, but the new regulations sought to expand and systematise their use. In particular, the workhouses were to be made deliberately harsh. This was in keeping with the Benthamite philosophy of Utilitarianism, which stated that, if offered a choice, people will always opt for the least unpleasant course of action. The threat of the workhouse, it was thought, would compel people to seek work rather than poor relief.

Unfortunately the Poor Law Commission of 1832, on whose findings the new legislation was based, had neglected to consider conditions in the newly industrialised areas of the North of England. Here workers and their families were more susceptible to temporary periods of unemployment caused by trade fluctuations, so the fear was that at such times entry into the dreaded workhouse would be inevitable. There was a

Milligan and Forbes warehouse, 1861 – magazine illustration. (Courtesy of Bradford Libraries)

trade slump in Bradford in 1837, so it was not surprising that people took to the streets, and the attack on the Court House was made by a crowd estimated to have been at least 5,000 strong. After the Riot Act was read a company of the 15th Hussars was dispatched from Leeds to deal with the mob, which was reluctant to disperse even when fired on. It was only when it started to rain heavily at about ten o'clock in the evening that the rioters began to go home.

In 1844 the so-called Orange riots occurred in Bradford. These were a reaction to the sudden arrival in the town of many Irish Catholics, displaced from their homeland because of the famine in Ireland. Chartist riots also took place in the 1840s (see Chapter Eight), but by the end of that decade a less violent era was at least in prospect, as the newly-formed corporation set about establishing some kind of order upon what had previously been a town suffering from an excess of unbridled and chaotic growth.

Squalor

According to the 1801 census the four areas that were to form the borough of Bradford after 1847 – Bradford, Horton, Manningham and Bowling – had a combined population of 13,364. This figure had risen to 26,309 by 1821 and to 66,715 by 1841. In 1851 the figure stood at 103,778. No other town in the country (with the possible exception of Middlesbrough) expanded at such a rate. Yet before 1847 there existed no effective mechanism for governing the town. The result was that in the first half of the nineteenth century Bradford became a byword for urban squalor. In 1844 James Smith wrote his famous description of Bradford in a report for the Health of Towns Commission: 'pools of slop water and filth are visible all over the surface. Dungheaps are found in several parts of the streets and open privies are seen in many directions. Large swill tubs are placed in various places by pig-feeders for collecting refuse from families ...' Smith was particularly struck by the filthy condition of Bradford Beck, in which people had been able to catch trout just fifty years earlier; and the canal, which had seemed to symbolise Bradford's entry into a bright new world of prosperity, had become little more than a cesspit:

> The chief sewerage, if sewerage it can be called, of the inferior streets and of the courts, is in the open channels and from the rough and unequal surface of the streets the flow is tardy and the whole soil is saturated with sewage water. The main sewage is discharged either into [Bradford Beck] or into the terminus or basin of the canal which runs into the lower part of the town. The water of this basin is often so charged with decaying matter that in the hot weather bubbles of hydrogen are continually rising to the surface and so much is the atmosphere loaded with that gas that watch-cases and other materials of silver become black in the pockets of workmen employed near the canal. The stench is sometimes very strong and fevers prevail much all around.

There had already been a serious outbreak of cholera in 1832 which had prompted the Vestry to forego its usual parsimony and allocate £300 towards the establishment of a hospital, but this action did not address the root cause of such epidemics – the all-pervading squalor in which many of Bradford's poorer families were now obliged to live. Smith summed up his inspection as follows: 'Taking the general condition of Bradford, I am obliged to pronounce it to be the most filthy town that I have visited and I see no symptoms of any improve-ment in the more recent arrangements for the abodes of the working classes.'

The Board of Surveyors, which was set up in 1843, presented a similar damn-ing report, especially concerning the disgraceful state of the canal and Bradford Beck:

> The drains of the town are emptied into this watercourse and principally above the floodgates. Besides, on the sides of the stream there are a great many factories of various kinds of manufacture, the soil, refuse and filth of which fall into the beck. In summer time the water is low, and all this filth

Right Newlands Mill disaster of 1882. (Courtesy of Bradford Libraries)

Below Newlands Mill disaster, magazine illustration. (Courtesy of Bradford Libraries)

accumulates for weeks, or months, above the floodgates and emits a most offensive smell. This noxious compound is conveyed through the sluice into the canal, where it undergoes a process which renders it still more offensive. For the mill owners below the floodgates, having a deficiency of water, contract with the proprietors of the canal for a supply of water for their boilers. The water is conveyed for this purpose in pipes to the boilers and, after being used for the generation of steam, is conveyed back again into the canal, so that the waters of the canal are scarcely ever cool in summer and constantly emit the most offensive gases.

Although the more prosperous inhabitants of Bradford were doubtless aware of the filthy nature of the canal – popularly known as 'River Stink' – they were able, if they chose, to ignore the horrible slum conditions of those living in areas such as Silsbridge Lane (now Grattan Road). Writing in 1836 in the *Bradford Observer*, James Burnley commented on this propensity for turning a blind eye: 'I wonder how many of the well-dressed, well-fed people, who daily pass up and down Westgate, have really any experience, or seriously consider, the wretchedness, the misery and the disease, of which the entrance to Silsbridge Lane is the threshold?'

The Improvement Commissioners

As early as the turn of the century some townspeople had had the foresight to realise that the Vestry meeting needed to be replaced. This body had proved itself to be ineffective in governing Bradford even when it was a small semi-rural township. In 1803 a group of prominent men successfully petitioned for an Improvement Act, which established a Board of Improvement Commissioners. The commissioners, fifty-eight in number, were responsible for the following: 'paving, lighting, watching and improving the town of Bradford and part of the hamlet of Little Horton, and for removing and preventing all nuisances therein'. The Board's activities were financed by rates levied on all townspeople occupying property of an annual value of at least £4. Only men with property worth £1,000 could become commissioners, and nobody who made his living from selling alcohol was permitted to serve. Unfortunately the Board did not actually replace the Vestry, which still continued to meet, retaining the right to oversee such things as poor relief and the surveying of certain streets and thoroughfares. It was noticeable too that the lord of the manor, Benjamin Rawson, chose not to become a commissioner, remaining aloof presumably because he thought that this new body would usurp whatever authority he still had. So from the start there was confusion over where power lay, and who was responsible for what. In addition the commissioners had no jurisdiction over nearby Bowling, Manningham and the bulk of Horton, all of which were about to experience the same kind of headlong expansion as Bradford. These three localities, which had a combined population of over 30,000 by the 1840s, lacked any kind of local government until they became part of the incorporated borough of Bradford in 1847.

Although it was set up in good faith, the Board of Improvement Commissioners was in reality almost as ineffectual as its predecessor. However, it could be said that as Bradford grew at such a prodigious rate during the first half of the century this is hardly surprising. As well as the unprecedented population growth, the sheer number of commercial and manufacturing concerns established in the vicinity would have created huge challenges for any kind of body attempting to make and enforce regulations for the town. In 1836 the Bradford Observer noted: 'The manufacturers are removing to Bradford as fast as they can get accommodated with looms.' By 1847 there were, by some estimates, eighty worsted mills, sixteen dyeworks, two hundred and fifty stuff and wool warehouses, forty collieries and twenty-two quarries. Regulations concerning such things as planning, building, pollution control and waste-management either did not exist or were ignored.

What might be considered laxity on the part of the Board of Commissioners was a result in part of its composition. The commissioners were drawn from Bradford's class of entrepreneurs and manufacturers. Consequently conflicts of interest were bound to arise, for whereas the Board members were charged with attempting to impose some kind of order and regulation on the town, as businessmen they were understandably reluctant to doing anything that might interfere with the successful expansion of their own commercial ventures. The commissioners were supposed to meet fortnightly, but there is evidence that the frequency of their meetings soon declined as members realised what a formidable task faced them, or perhaps they simply lost interest. In 1817, for example, the commissioners do not appear to have met at all.

Did the commissioners achieve anything? A few examples will indicate their impact (or lack of it). It is important to note that rather than employing people directly they usually outsourced work to private contractors, a practice that has in more recent times once more become fashionable in local and national government circles alike. In 1805, in an attempt to fulfil their duty to keep the streets clean, the commissioners contracted with William Jowett, at a rate of £10 a year, for him to cleanse the streets twice a week. It seems that this arrangement did not work and it was superseded by one that aimed to use able-bodied paupers as street cleaners. However, the Guardians of the Poor wanted a price that the Commissioners were unwilling to pay, so the scheme fell through, provoking a contemporary writer to describe the filth of Bradford's streets using the following comparison: '[the streets would] disgrace a Hottentot settlement.'

The commissioners were also supposed to attend to street lighting, and this was one area where they could be said to have had a measure of success. They duly employed three lamplighters, each to be paid 10s 6d a week to light some streets in the town centre. In the early years of the century the lamps used oil, but in 1821 the commissioners contracted with the newly formed Bradford Gaslight Company to light streets from Vicar Lane and the bottom of Leeds Road right through the town to Westgate, North Parade and part of Manningham Lane.

The Commissioners were also supposed to make provision for this same area of town-centre streets to be watched. Originally seven watchmen were appointed at 12s per week each, with a Christmas bonus of half a guinea. This provision proved totally inadequate, and in 1831 the Vestry – rather usurping one of the functions of the commissioners – followed the example of Leeds and Manchester and established the Bradford Police. This consisted of a head of police, with a salary of £150 a year, a vagrant master, paid £50 a year, and a deputy-constable, who had no salary but would receive instead the fees for executing warrants and serving summonses. An early holder of this third post was not slow, apparently, to use a stout blackthorn cudgel to enforce the law. Some special constables were also recruited so that the Bradford Police could ensure the following: 'repression of the irregularities and multiplied offences which are daily perpetrated, to the disgrace of our civic character, and to the mortification of all correct and proper feeling.'

In the years 1832-34 the force managed to apprehend 238 disorderly persons and 293 vagrants; 270 felons were arrested, of whom no fewer than fifty-five were sentenced to transportation.

Bradford is incorporated

As the mid-point of the century approached it was obvious that neither the archaic Vestry meeting nor a body like the Board of Improvement Commissioners was fit for the purpose of governing Bradford. Many towns-people continued to ignore whatever regulations were promulgated by the commissioners. For example, in 1825 the Board made the following resolution: 'That the hog-sty in Manningham Lane opposite Christ Church, and the muck-heap opposite Rawson Place be removed, and that Thomas Hoadley's pigs be not allowed to run loose and be fed in the Market Place.' We do not

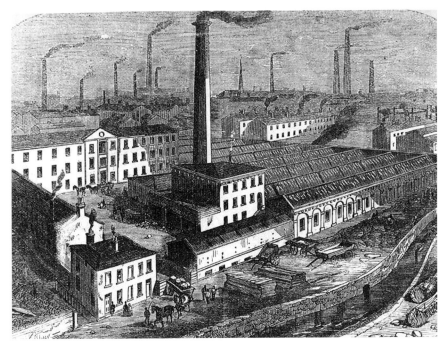

Beehive Mills and vista of chimneys. (Courtesy of Bradford Libraries)

know if Thomas Hoadley obeyed this injunction to control his pigs; certainly the commissioners had few sanctions available to compel him to do so. Nor did they really have any way of compelling the owner of the hog-sty (probably Hoadley again) to demolish it. Likewise, in the 1840s there were reports that workmen employed by the Board of Surveyors were in some cases threatened or driven off when they approached some properties, the owners of which saw no good reason for their presence. In short, the Board of Improvement Commissioners, the Board of Surveyors and the Vestry were all as toothless as they were ineffective.

Following the Reform Act of 1832 those now eligible to vote elected Bradford's first two MPs, Cunliffe Lister and John Hardy. In 1835 the Municipal Corporation Act was passed, which allowed large urban areas, such as Bradford, to establish a more democratic and efficient system of local government via a charter of incorporation. After various false-starts the Privy Council was petitioned in 1845 by one group of Bradford's leading citizens and a counter-petition was presented by a second group. Bizarrely, some people signed both. The Improvement Commissioners were split, thirty-two being in favour of incorporation and the rest opposed to it. This led to much acrimony, and the commissioners passed the following strongly worded resolution in May 1845: 'That the Commissioners present, having heard with feeling of indignation the memorial addressed by some of their number to the Privy Council against a Charter of Incorporation ... declare that a majority of the Commissioners who signed the memorial have, by their notorious inattention to the duties of office, rendered themselves ineligible to give an opinion on the question.' The vicar of Bradford was opposed to incorporation, probably fearing it would lead to his losing influence in the town, and some manufacturers were opposed, because they suspected that substantial rates would be demanded of them to pay for the new regime. Local Tories, always suspicious in those days of any moves to extend the franchise or embrace democracy, were also opposed.

In 1846 a second petition was presented. This one indicated much more support for incorporation, and in 1847 Bradford gained its new status as an incorporated borough. The township was duly divided into four wards, rather unimaginatively designated North, South, East and West. Manningham, Great Horton, Little Horton and Bowling also became wards of the new borough. There were to be fourteen aldermen and forty-two councillors, each of whom had to own property of at least £1,000 to qualify, and the franchise was to consist of all males who were householders. Bradford's first mayor was Robert Milligan, a Scot who had settled in Bradford in 1810 and had subsequently become a leading stuff (textile) merchant. Like many who were to follow him in the early days of the mayoralty, Milligan was a staunch Liberal.

Bradford now had a corporation. It also had a railway line, opened in 1846, linking it with Leeds and thence to the rest of the country. By 1850 it had a somewhat cleaner water supply, after the springs at Manywells, near Wilsden, were connected by pipes to feed the town via reservoirs at Chellow and Whetley Hill. Bradford's first public park was opened soon afterwards, named after the great supporter of free trade, Sir Robert Peel. And featured on the town's brand new coat of arms was the legendary boar without a tongue, that early symbol of Bradford's identity referred to in Chapter One. After half a century of squalor and near-chaos, things were perhaps beginning to look up.

five

GERMAN AND IRISH CONNECTIONS

The natives of Scotland are here, the natives of Ireland are here, from the pleasant vales of Devonshire men and women have come: from the banks of the Rhine and the Elbe they are coming.

> Revd Jonathan Glyde, Minister at Horton Lane
> Congregational Chapel, 1835-54

Bradford has traditionally been a destination for immigrants, and a later chapter will examine the impact that more recent arrivals have had on the city. In the mid-nineteenth century two very different groups of newcomers arrived in Bradford from overseas: Irish men and women seeking to escape from destitution and the terrible famine of the 1840s, and German merchants out to make their fortunes from Bradford's booming textile trade.

The German merchants

> It was some time before the trade in general learned the lesson of their example ... the English wool trade in its expansion to every corner of the world owed a great deal to the German merchants who introduced efficient distribution and businesslike terms of payment in place of chance sales and haphazard settlement.
>
> Memoirs of Sir Jacob Behrens

Throughout the nineteenth and early twentieth centuries almost five million Germans left their native land, most of them settling in the USA. According to the census of 1851 there were about 250 foreigners, mainly from north Germany, residing in Bradford. They were a small but highly influential group who had come to the town from the 1830s onwards. The first we have any real knowledge of was Leo Schuster, who was trading in the town as a stuff merchant in 1829. He was followed by others in the 1830s and 1840s, so that twenty-four of the fifty-two stuff merchants operating in Bradford were German by 1845 and 40 per cent of worsteds produced in Bradford bore German names by 1861. It is important to understand that the Germans in Bradford were not textile manufacturers, like Salt or Lister (see Chapter Seven); they were traders. The *Yorkshire Observer*, in an article written in the mid-twentieth century, described them thus: 'Their great forte was not a technical one. They knew very little about the manufacturing side of the industry, but they allied their powers as salesmen to the prowess of their Yorkshire colleagues as craftsmen, and between the two of them Bradford captured the markets of the world.'

What brought the German merchants to Bradford was the opportunity to make money from exporting textiles to the Continent, especially to Germany, which was the main European market at that time. Jacob Behrens was one of the most important of these men. Originally from Hamburg, he came to Bradford in 1838 and in his memoirs produced this rationale for coming to the town: 'The commission merchant on the spot in England, buying for foreign customers with expert knowledge and at market prices, had obvious advantages over the stock-holding merchant on the Continent.'

Behrens was responsible for founding the Bradford Chamber of Commerce in 1851 and for the next thirty years – the heyday of the worsted trade in Bradford – German merchants accounted for about a quarter of the subscribers to the Chamber. In a tribute to Behrens on his death in 1889, the *Bradford Observer* commented: 'He was representative ... of the essentials, of the varied qualities which have made the town what it is commercially and socially.' In another obituary, the *Illustrated Weekly Telegraph* said: 'Bradford is indebted to Behrens more than any other man for the bringing into life of the Chamber of Commerce and giving it not only importance among the mercantile community but weight and influence with the

Kessler's warehouse, Vicar Lane, 1886. (Courtesy of Bradford Libraries)

government on mercantile matters.' Behrens received a knighthood in 1882 in recognition of his work in promoting exports and the influence he had in shaping the policies of the Board of Trade. He also had the foresight to realise that if Bradford's commercial success was to be sustained its trade and industry had to be led by well-educated managers, and to this end he was instrumental in reorganising Bradford Grammar School in 1871 and establishing Bradford Technical College in 1882.

Rothenstein and Falkenheim's warehouses, Vicar Lane. (Courtesy of Bradford Libraries)

The German merchants opened their first warehouses in the centre of the town. Schuster opened his in Hall Ings in 1845, and Steinthal followed him with one in Charles Street in 1856. Both merchants relocated their premises to the Vicar Lane and Leeds Road area in the 1860s, and before long the impressive Italianate warehouses in what was to become Little Germany were being constructed. By 1880 over twenty of these were operating, including Caspian House in East Parade, the premises of Messrs Delius and Company. This contained showrooms, a stockroom and a counting house. The merchant's quarter of Little Germany contributed to a textile trade in Bradford that increased in worth from an estimated £500,000 in 1829 to about £32 million in 1869. In his *History of the Worsted Trade in England from the Earliest Times*, published in 1857, John James comments as follows on the role and influence of the Germans: 'These merchants ... are a large and respectable colony in Bradford; [they] have become part and parcel of our society; are interested in the success of our trade and heartily seek to maintain our prosperity. To them, in seasons of depression, much has been owing; with judicious enterprise they have, on such occasions, bought largely for the future and thus rendered efficient aid in times of difficulty and pressure.' James is correct in describing the German colony as respectable, but it was never particularly large. However, the influence of the German merchants and the contribution they made to Bradford in the nineteenth century went far beyond their actual numbers. And this contribution extended into the political life of the town. After a time German merchants became town councillors and aldermen. Charles Semon was Mayor in 1864-66 and Jacob Moser was Lord Mayor in 1910-11. Moser became a freeman of the city in 1908 and reputedly contributed £30,000 to charity.

In *English Journey* (1934) J.B. Priestley refers to the German colony as being Jewish, but in fact the community was made up of Gentiles as well as Jews. The Deutsche Evangelische Kirche (now the home of the Delius Centre) opened in Great Horton Road in 1882. It cost £3,150 to build and benefited from contributions from the Kaiser and the King of Bavaria. By the end of the nineteenth century this Protestant church had rather more than 100 members. The German Jewish community was larger. A synagogue was opened in Bowland Street in 1881 and soon had 200-300 members. It is reputed to have been one of only two purpose-built Jewish places of worship in Britain outside London at that time. Interestingly, some Jews attended services at Bradford's Unitarian church, presumably because they found that the Unitarians, who do not adhere to the doctrine of the Trinity or believe in the divinity of Jesus, were not too distant from the Jewish religious tradition.

The German community also contributed much to Bradford's cultural life, establishing literary societies and supporting such bodies as the Bradford Festival Choral Society. Close links were made with the Hallé Orchestra and an annual season of subscription concerts was established. But perhaps the greatest contribution to the culture of their adopted land lay in the Germans' offspring, some of whom would become famous artists, writers and composers.

Frederick Delius

In her book *Memories of my Brother*, published in 1935, Clare Delius writes:

> Julius Delius's business was to buy and sell wool and the fact that he had brought with him some engaging qualities of his national culture – a love of music amongst them – did not deflect him from the main object of his emigration. He was in Bradford, and in exile, not for his health, as the phrase is, but to make money out of wool. Dominant by nature, pursuing this idea with German thoroughness, he prospered exceedingly.

No doubt the other German merchants were like Julius Delius; in self-imposed exile with the sole aim of accumulating wealth. But if their children had artis-

tic talents rather than a commercial bent, then life in Bradford and a career in textiles might well have been seen as things to escape from as soon as possible.

Frederick Delius (1862-1934) was born in Bradford and educated at Bradford Grammar School, where he was a contemporary of John Coates, who later became a well-known

Deutsche Evangelische Kirche / Delius Centre. (Sue Naylor)

opera singer. Although Julius, according to Clare's account, had a great love of music, his intention was for his son to join the family firm of wool merchants in Bradford, a career for which Frederick had neither interest nor aptitude. He was sent to Florida in 1884 to manage an orange plantation, but this was not a success. Eventually Julius must have realised the futility of trying to stand in the way of his son's musical ambitions, and in 1886 Frederick enrolled at the Leipzig Conservatoire, after which he lived in Paris. While he was there he met the playwright August Strindberg and the artists Paul Gauguin and Edvard Munch. He also caught syphilis.

By the early twentieth century Delius had become famous, especially after his work was promoted by the conductor Sir Thomas Beecham (another who had rejected the family firm in favour of a musical career), and today he is recognised as a major composer of the early twentieth century. For much of his life he lived in Grez-sur-Loing in France, where he died in 1934, blind and paralysed from the effects of the tertiary stage of syphilis. As far as is known he never came back to Bradford, although he was made a free-man of the city in 1932. The honour was bestowed on him in Grez by a party of Bradford's civic dignitaries who travelled to France for the occasion. Delius expressed the following wish for his burial place: 'Some country churchyard in the south of England where people could place wild flowers.' Consequently he was buried in the village of Limpsfield, Surrey, rather than in his native city. However, despite a reluctance to return to his birthplace he never lost his Yorkshire accent, according to the music critic Neville Cardus, and even though most of his life was spent in France he retained a strong interest in cricket, a game that he had played with enthusiasm as a youth in Bradford.

William Rothenstein

Like Julius Delius, Moritz Rothenstein came to Bradford (in 1859) from Germany to make money from the town's booming textile trade. And just like Julius's son, Frederick, Moritz's son William (1872-1945) rejected the idea of entering his father's woollen business after leaving Bradford Grammar School. Instead he went to study at the Slade School of Art in London, followed by three years in Paris, where he met James McNeil Whistler, Edgar Degas and Henri Toulouse-Lautrec. Rothenstein returned to London in 1893 and developed a reputation as a portrait painter – the National Portrait Gallery possesses 200 of his portraits. In both world wars he was an official war artist and from 1920 to 1935 he was the principal of the Royal College of Art. Henry Moore, born in 1898 in Castleford, just down the road from Bradford, was one of Rothenstein's students, and he made the following comment about Rothenstein's influence and, incidentally, about the need that the person from the provinces often has for a confidence-boost before he or she can proceed to a wider stage: '[Rothenstein] gave me the feeling that there was no barrier, no limit to what a young provincial artist could get to be and do.'

It would seem that Delius and Rothenstein, probably because they came from wealthy immigrant families, never felt any of Moore's provincial uncertainty. Bradford produced them and provided an education and a comfortable upbringing, after which they moved almost seamlessly away from their provincial background and into international recognition. Like their fathers, the German merchants of Bradford, they were essentially citizens of the world.

Humbert Wolfe

In his autobiographical work *Now a Stranger*, published in 1933, the poet Humbert Wolfe describes his early life as a member of Bradford's German-Jewish community. Wolfe was born in Milan but spent his childhood in Bradford where his father, Martin, was a worsted merchant. Of particular interest in the book is Wolfe's description of the family home and its immediate neighbourhood. He paints a rather idyllic picture of his formative years in Manningham, the Bradford suburb where many members of the city's wealthier class had their homes in the 1890s. The Wolfes lived in Mount Royd, which at that time was an exclusive enclave. With its own private communal gardens

it was really a nineteenth-century version of a gated community, close to the busy thoroughfare of Manningham Lane. The Wolfes' neighbours in Mount Royd included other textile merchants, as well as doctors, lawyers and a colonel in the militia. Most of them were members of Bradford's German community. Wolfe appears to have had a happy childhood, playing cricket in the gardens of Mount Royd and enjoying the delights of nearby Lister Park. In the 1920s – by which time he had, perhaps predictably, moved away from Bradford – he became well known as a poet, and was even tipped to become Poet Laureate when Robert Bridges died in 1930. Today the only lines of Wolfe's that might be remembered are these:

> You cannot hope to bribe or twist
> Thank God! The British journalist,
> But, seeing what the man will do
> Unbribed, there's no occasion to.

Jewish Reform Synagogue, Bowland Street.
(Courtesy of Bradford Libraries)

4, Mount Royd, childhood home of Humbert Wolfe, poet. (Sue Naylor)

Some may feel that this epigram of Wolfe's has a certain contemporary relevance in view of twenty-first-century revelations about illegalities perpetrated by some journalists, and government investigations into corrupt practices within the press.

The Irish

It would only have been a fifteen-minute walk from Wolfe's genteel haven in Mount Royd to the White Abbey and Goitside areas of Bradford where many Irish immigrants had settled, though it is doubtful whether Wolfe would ever have made such a trip. If he had done so he would have entered a completely different world.

Although there had been a tradition of seasonal migration from Ireland to England, the hardships experienced by thousands of Irish people because of famine in the 1840s led to a massive amount of permanent emigration. Many immigrants arrived in Bradford from County Mayo and County Sligo in the

west of Ireland, but a significant number also came from Queen's County (now County Laois). There was a particular reason for this. Some towns in Queen's County had developed as centres for cloth manufacturing. Mount Mellick was the most important of these, and in the early nineteenth century it had even been dubbed (rather grandiloquently) the Manchester of Ireland. Cloth manufacturing was carried on predominantly as a cottage industry, although one or two steam-powered mills were built in the first decades of the nineteenth century. An increase in Ireland's population in the eighteenth century had meant that before long there was not enough good agricultural land to sustain the growing numbers, so just as in the Bradford area many families took up combing, spinning and weaving to supplement the income they derived from farming. Even before the catastrophic famine years of the 1840s people were leaving Queen's County, and because many people from Mount Mellick and the neighbouring towns had experience of textile manufacturing it was natural for them, when times became hard, to come and seek work in Bradford, with its booming textile-based economy.

The population of Mount Mellick declined by 35 per cent between 1845 and 1850. Meanwhile the Irish community in Bradford increased. According to the 1841 census about 5 per cent of the population of the township of Bradford was originally from Ireland. By 1851 this had increased to 8 per cent. With a significant number of Irish immigrants in Keighley, the total for the wider Bradford area was probably around 10,000 by the middle of the century. Bradford itself attracted more immigrants from Ireland than any other Yorkshire town at this period.

These newcomers settled in the poorest parts of the town, such as White Abbey and notably Goitside, where the 1851 census revealed that at least 2,300 Irish people were crammed into the small area bounded by Westgate, Southgate, Thornton Road and Silsbridge Lane (now Grattan Road), a density of about 800 people per acre. This level of over-crowding in unsanitary slums led to appalling living conditions. Thus in Thompson's Buildings ninety-five people shared eight rooms and in 1845 thirty-three people were reported to be sharing seven beds in Mill Bank (close to where Sunbridge Road is now). One of Titus Salt's earlier mills was close to Goitside, and witnessing these terrible living conditions helped stimulate his desire to create the model village of Saltaire (see Chapter Seven). In 1845 the *Bradford Observer* reported on the living conditions of the Irish: 'a revealing description of the crowded state of the houses and sleeping apartments and the mode in which both sexes are

St Patrick's RC Church, off Westgate. (Sue Naylor)

huddled together regardless of morality or decency'. In a further report that year, referring to domestic wool combing in the Irish community, the *Bradford Observer* stated: 'Houses are generally overcrowded with men and women working together indiscriminately. The back parts of the street on both sides have filthy yards and cellars in which the inmates are crowded together. Several children have died of fever in the last few weeks.'

In 1865 it was reported that in the worst streets forty people were sharing one privy and pigs were kept in some of the yards. Infant mortality was generally high in nineteenth-century Bradford, at 200 deaths per 1,000 live births in 1872 and 181 per 1,000 in 1881, but the infant mortality rate in the Irish ghettoes was even higher. Scarlet fever, a life-threatening disease for children in the days before antibiotics, was particularly rife, as was tuberculosis.

The Irish immigrants had come from acute hardship and poverty in Ireland only to find it again in Bradford. Although work was usually available pay was low, and rents, even in slum areas like Goitside, were comparatively high, even for a shared bed. In vivid contrast to the highly educated and cultured members of Bradford's German community, the Irish immigrants were often illiterate. According to the 1841 Irish census 79 per cent of the population of the western counties – from which many of Bradford's immigrants came – were unable to read and write. Many spoke no English, leading to the following request in 1865 for priests to come to Bradford: '[Men who] could

Irish Club, Rebecca Street. (Sue Naylor)

speak the language of the Celt to hear the confession of the Faithful who have no English.'

In the 1840s one seventh of the Irish immigrants were involved in domestic wool combing, but Lister's patented wool combing machine was fast eliminating the need for this work. Other immigrants worked as hawkers and pedlars; over 80 per cent of people earning a living by such means in Bradford in 1851 were from the Irish community. There were virtually no members of the professional or clerical classes drawn from the Irish at this time.

A sizeable number found work as builders' labourers, a ready source of employment during the building boom in Bradford. Certainly Irish labour helped build the Town Hall in the 1870s, but when it came to placing the statue of Oliver Cromwell on the façade of the building alongside the effigies of all the English monarchs a problem arose. Cromwell had been a detested figure among the Irish for over 200 years because of the atrocities he perpetrated in Ireland, notably the massacre of the garrison at Drogheda in 1649. Bradford Corporation officials learned that the gang of Irish labourers who were scheduled to lift Cromwell's statue into place were planning to fake an accident and let the statue drop to the ground, where it would have been smashed to pieces. To prevent this from happening the Irish labourers were given a day's holiday, and the task of hoisting the statue into place was allocated to a group of English labourers who, presumably, felt no animosity towards Cromwell. The statue remains in place today.

Not surprisingly the poverty and terrible living conditions that the Irish immigrants had to endure often led to antisocial behaviour and delinquency. Drunkenness, assaults on the police and brawling in the streets were particular problems. In 1851 the *Bradford Observer* noted the incidence of faction fighting – mass brawls between rival gangs or between families struggling to assert themselves: 'We understand that the low Irish residents in this town manifest at the present time unusual symptoms of pugnacity. There is a disposition to indulge in faction fights.'

In 1862 a total of 954 arrests were made in the town, 272 of which involved Irish immigrants. In the years between 1860 and 1890, although the proportion of Irish people in Bradford was never much greater than 8 per cent, the number brought before the magistrates was disproportionately high, never less than 14 per cent of the total, rising in some years to 24 per cent.

The Irish came from an impoverished, rural and Catholic background. They were trying to settle into an urban, largely Protestant environment with a different culture. Some friction was inevitable; the Irish were generally very much looked down upon by the other townspeople. English mill-workers resented the Irish workers' readiness to work for lower wages and, at times, act as strike-breakers. This rather sardonic report from the *Bradford Observer* on the occasion of Queen Victoria's Coronation celebrations in 1838 captures some of the scorn felt for the Irish in the early years of migration. It also hints at the potential for inter-communal strife: 'The most extraordinary feature of the procession was the Catholic and Orange Societies forming part of the same procession without falling out in any way. It has been stated that such an occurrence has not been known since the Battle of the Boyne.'

As one would expect churches were an important focus for the Irish immigrants. St Mary's was built as early as 1825 to serve the community in the Barkerend Road area and five more were built in the nineteenth century, including St Patrick's in Sedgefield Terrace, which served the communities in Goitside and White Abbey. Because of anti-Catholic feeling in the town, the purchase of the land for St Patrick's was undertaken in some secrecy, with go-betweens being used to hide the identity of the purchasers. In his *Records and Reminiscences of St Patrick's Parish* (1903), J. Earnshaw describes the reaction to this subterfuge: 'Great was the wrath of the vendors, Misses Mary and Elizabeth Rawson, when they found that the land was to be used for the erection of a Catholic church.'

Sixteen more Catholic churches were built in the twentieth century, most of these near to the council estates where the Irish Catholics were re-housed once

slum clearance began. In 1909 Bradford Council established the Longlands Improvement Area, which led to the city's earliest municipal housing projects in Longlands Street, Chain Street and a little later in nearby Wigan Street. The majority of these new houses were occupied by members of the Irish community who had previously lived in the slums of Goitside and White Abbey. By this time the wretched slum dwellings of Goitside had been demolished and industrial premises and warehouses had been built in their place.

Clubs associated with the Irish Democratic League were founded, normally one in each parish and named after notable Irish republicans. Thus St Mary's parish had the Wolfe Tone Club, St Peter's the Michael Davitt Club, and so on. The Irish Self Determination League had its North of England headquarters at the Turks Head Hotel in Birksland Street, off Leeds Road. These organisations were naturally strong supporters of the Irish independence movement, especially at the time of the Irish rebellion in the early 1920s. The Catholic clergy did not necessarily stay neutral. It is said that a cache of guns and ammunition was hidden in the loft of St Mary's presbytery during this period. Years later, in 1945, when he was on the run from the British authorities because of his IRA activities, Brendan Behan was given shelter for a couple of nights in a safe house in Bradford's Irish community. His brief stay is described in his book *Confessions of an Irish Rebel* (1965). Behan was to become the most well-known Irish playwright of the mid-twentieth century, lionised in the USA and Britain as well as in his native Ireland.

Two contrasting communities

The German merchants, comparatively small in number, had a profound effect on Bradford. They helped to position the town alongside those throughout the North and Midlands that produced the wealth to make Britain the dominant country in the world in the nineteenth century. Furthermore, what J.B. Priestley refers to as a German-Jewish cultural leavening made Bradford, for a time, something of a European as well as a provincial English city. The pity was that, after the catastrophe of the First World War, little of the German community and its influence remained to help sustain Bradford's progress.

Unlike the German merchants, the Irish came and stayed. Their importance in the story of Bradford lies not so much in their commercial or cultural contribution to the city in Victorian times, although they did – quite literally – build much of Bradford; rather they stand as an example of how it is possible for the members of a large immigrant group to overcome severe hardship and prejudice and make their way in a foreign land. The Irish founded their own churches and, importantly, their own Catholic schools so that their children would be well-educated and able to join mainstream British society without losing a sense of their heritage. Businesses developed and, as time went on, people from an Irish background entered the city's professional and commercial life. Like the Germans before them, members of the Irish community also began to enter local politics, and eventually some gained high civic office. Integration into the life of the city was eventually achieved, and thus was begun Bradford's tradition of receiving large numbers of overseas immigrants. Each of the groups that were to follow the Irish and settle in Bradford in the twentieth century would face barriers of various kinds, but with time, self-help and the right kind of support from the municipal authorities, it would be possible to overcome many of the problems. Bradford's Irish community had shown the way.

six

BOOM TOWN

Bradford Comes of Age

One of the low on whom assurance sits
As a silk hat on a Bradford millionaire.

T. S. Eliot (1888-1965)

This is a quotation from *The Wasteland*, usually regarded as one of the most influential poems of the twentieth century. It was written in 1922, when Bradford's fortunes had already begun to decline, yet the allusion to millionaires in the town would still have been clear enough. From the 1850s right up to the outbreak of the First World War Bradford was associated with great wealth derived from its textile industry and trade. In the years immediately preceding 1914, though its riches were far from being evenly distributed, Bradford was nonetheless estimated by some economists to be the wealthiest city in Europe. It was a place to be reckoned with. Rather sadly this is no longer the case, and present-day students of English literature may well find the reference to Bradford millionaires in Eliot's poem somewhat puzzling.

Bradford's development in the second half of the nineteenth century into one of Britain's most successful cities – in commercial terms at least – could not have happened if the haphazard and unregulated growth that had characterised the town before 1850 had been allowed to continue. Bradford might well have drowned in its own filth. Even in 1866, when some efforts at regulation were being made, the River Aire and Bradford Beck were still a disgrace. Giving evidence to the government's Rivers Commission in that year, Henry Mitchell, a stuff merchant of Leeds Road and a future Mayor of Bradford, made the following comments about the Aire at Esholt, 5 miles from the centre of Bradford: 'It is very filthy and very bad ... the [filth] arises chiefly from the Bradford Beck, also from several mills and factories on the river and partly from Shipley ... the [colour of the water] is almost black sometimes ... it is very offensive.'

St George's Hall, lunch for Prince of Wales. 1904, from a magazine illustration. (Courtesy of Bradford Libraries)

Once Bradford was incorporated in 1847 and had a town council, the way was clear for improvements to be made, and while it would still be many years before pollution of the Aire and Bradford Beck was properly tackled, other vital issues facing the Corporation began to be addressed – and really for the first time. There was certainly much to be done.

Law and order

In the 1840s – a very troubled time for Bradford – the town was not only disease-ridden and filthy, it was also the scene of much lawlessness, drunkenness and prostitution. In 1843 the *Bradford Observer* commented: '[Bradford is] infested with thieves and vagabonds, the doors of its inhabitants besieged with beggars, whilst riot, drunkenness and street-fighting is carried on with impunity.' Titus Salt, who was mayor in 1848 and 1849, commissioned an enquiry into the moral condition of the town and this reported as follows in 1850: 'Considerably more than 150 beershops exist in the borough and ... scarcely any of them can be described as being decent and orderly houses of entertainment ... Facilities

Town Hall Square, visit of Prince of Wales, 1904. (Courtesy of Bradford Libraries)

for dishonourable intercourse between the sexes are afforded by almost all and some are in fact brothels under another name.'

One of the new Corporation's first acts was to establish a more efficient police force, just in time to deal with the Chartist riots of 1848. This new force had a well-paid (£250 a year) chief constable, who by the mid-1850s was leading a force of over 100 officers. No doubt this body helped to create a more law-abiding town, but there were instances of violence against policemen in the early years, the most famous being in 1857 when an unpopular constable was beaten by a mob and then paraded naked round the public houses in Wibsey. Drunkenness on duty could be a problem too; in the 1870s 10 per cent of the force had to be disciplined for this misdemeanour. And in 1855 the police, probably wisely, turned a blind eye to an outbreak of particularly boisterous drunkenness in the streets when people celebrated the fall of Sebastopol in the Crimean War. The passing of the 1868 Beer Bill enabled ninety of the worst-conducted public houses to be closed.

Throughout the century the members of the Town Council and the Watch Committee were, in the main, drawn from Bradford's elite class of businessmen. Consequently, at times of industrial unrest the police force tended to be used as a tool of the employers. This was particularly apparent in the Manningham Mills dispute of 1891-92, when the police and the Watch Committee attracted much criticism for the way they attempted to curb the strikers' meetings and demonstrations (see Chapter Eight).

Improving the town

In 1850 the Bradford Improvement Act became law, but not before some very heated debates among Bradford's councillors, one of whom called the Improvement Bill that preceded the Act 'the greatest swindle ever practised upon a Committee of the House of Commons'. Cudworth, in his *Historical Notes on the Bradford Corporation*, states: 'The progress of the Bill through Parliament was diversified at home by scenes in the Council chamber which would have disgraced a pot-house.' As with the debate that had accompanied Bradford's incorporation three years earlier, opposition to the Improvement Bill was all about money and the fear that increases in the rates were in the offing – there was frequently a reluctance on the part of some prominent men of the town to contribute to the public purse from their own often very deep pockets. Nevertheless, the powers derived from the Act enabled the Corporation to start on the huge task of improvement. In an attempt to ameliorate the conditions in which many poor people lived, the building of back-to-back houses was banned in 1854 (only to be permitted again in 1865, before being finally banned in 1873). Before building regulations were introduced in 1854 there was, according to Cudworth: 'no restriction or restraint whatever upon the operations of builders of dwelling houses, which ... were almost invariably crowded together into the least possible space, and with the least possible convenience, in order to produce a maximum of rent for a minimum of outlay'.

It has been estimated that in the late 1850s almost three-quarters of all houses in Bradford were back-to-back. In the 1870s cellar dwellings, in which many families lived in shockingly unsanitary and overcrowded conditions, were banned. It was made illegal in 1875 for any dwelling to be constructed unless it had drainage and a couple of years later many of the dreadful slums in the Silsbridge Lane (now Grattan Road) area were demolished. The Housing and Working Classes Act of 1890 extended the Corporation's powers to demolish inadequate houses, but re-housing people from slum areas was not necessarily seen as a Corporation priority and it was not until 1909 that the first municipal

Darley Street, late nineteenth century. (Courtesy of Bradford Libraries)

housing scheme was completed in the Longlands area, after much urging by
Fred Jowett, Bradford's first Labour MP.

Bradford seems to have been gripped by a building mania between 1850 and
the end of the century. In 1851-52 plans were made for ninety-four new streets,
1,340 dwelling houses, thirty-one mills and warehouses, eighty-four shops,
eleven churches, chapels and schools and no fewer than 237 miscellaneous
buildings. In 1874 plans were made for 1,860 houses, sixty-seven warehouses
and mills, seven chapels and churches, four public buildings and 253 miscellaneous buildings. Clearly there was a need for these new buildings, especially
the houses, for while in 1851 the population of the town was 103,778, just
twenty years later it was 147,101. It had risen to 279,767 by 1901.

Public buildings and the growth of civic pride

In 1853 St George's Hall was opened, at a cost of £20,000 raised by private subscription. It was Bradford's first purpose-built civic building and
the Council met there every month until the Town Hall was completed in
1873. From the start it also functioned as a concert hall and as a venue for
lectures and public meetings. Charles Dickens reputedly read instalments of

Bleak House to a packed audience in the hall in the year following its opening and in 1910 Winston Churchill was attacked at a political meeting by a group of suffragettes who had hidden beneath the stage. (In another version of this story it was Churchill who had to take refuge under the stage to escape the women.) St George's Hall is reputedly the oldest concert hall still in regular use in Britain.

In 1859, the editor of the *Bradford Observer* felt able to report that good progress was being made in promoting some degree of civic pride among the townspeople: 'It used to be a reproach against us that Bradford was a settlement rather than a community ... of late years we have been proud to see an "esprit de corps" unknown before, diffusing itself among us with justifiable pride on the part of the inhabitants in their fellow townsmen and in their town.'

Two other major public buildings followed the construction of St George's Hall: the Wool Exchange and the Town Hall. The Wool Exchange, which replaced the Piece Hall, had its foundation stone laid by Lord Palmerston in 1864. By now the Corporation and Bradford's leading businessmen (usually, of course, the same people) were so imbued with municipal self-confidence that they organised an event which verged on the outrageous in its pomp and circumstance. Church bells were rung, flags were flown and there was a nineteen-gun salute in Peel Park. Approximately 100 carriages, attended by two military bands, drove in procession from Peel Park to the site of the Exchange on Market Street. In the evening Palmerston was the guest of the Corporation at a grand dinner held in St George's Hall, where the Bradford Choral Society greeted him with a rendition of 'See the Conquering Hero Comes'. The only fly in the ointment, apparently, was a demonstration by a large number of working men in the streets of the town who steadfastly refused to cheer the distinguished visitor. Their silent protest was because of Palmerston's stubborn refusal to countenance an extension of the franchise.

The foundation stone of Bradford Town Hall (now usually called City Hall) was laid in 1870. Like St George's Hall and the Wool Exchange the design of the Town Hall was the brainchild of local architects Lockwood and Mawson, who also designed Kirkgate Market (opened in 1872) and the whole of Saltaire. In fact Lockwood and Mawson won so many of the competitions for designing prestigious buildings in Bradford at this time that some people began to suspect that the competitions were rigged. Be that as it may, Lockwood and Mawson designed some magnificent buildings and those that remain can still be admired in the twenty-first century.

Town Hall, laying the foundation stone, 1870. (Courtesy of Bradford Libraries)

The Town Hall has a Gothic façade and a clock tower which is a copy of the campanile of the Palazzo Vecchio in Florence, perhaps indicating that by this stage the Corporation and the architects could see a parallel between the centre of the Italian Renaissance and the centre of Britain's wealth-creating worsted trade. The Town Hall ranks with that of Manchester and Leeds as a prime example of Victorian civic pride. In the same decade many of the warehouses in what is now called Little Germany were built. Although these were commercial rather than public buildings, the elegance of their design – again often a palazzo style influenced by the Italian Renaissance – gives further evidence of Bradford's self-awareness as a major commercial centre.

Other fine buildings were constructed later, including Bradford's art gallery, Cartwright Hall, opened in Lister Park by the Prince of Wales in 1904. Somewhat earlier Swan Arcade was completed in 1877 on the site of the former White Swan Inn. J.B. Priestley had his first job in the office of a wool merchant in Swan Arcade and he (with many others) was incensed when the arcade was demolished in the 1960s as part of a so-called modernisation scheme that involved needlessly tearing down many of Bradford's impressive Victorian buildings.

Improving public health: water and waste

The town urgently needed more than civic pride and elegant public buildings. There had to be an investment in public health, particularly in two key areas: the provision of an adequate and clean water supply and an efficient sewerage system. In 1855 the Corporation bought out the private company that had previously supplied the town with water. The plan was to pipe water from the Worth Valley, which runs between Keighley and Haworth, but objections from mill owners in that area hampered this, so the Corporation was obliged to go further afield and over the next few years reservoirs were built in Airedale and Wharfedale, the most distant being those at Grimwith and Barden, some way beyond Bolton Abbey and 20 miles from the centre of Bradford. By 1864 there were eleven reservoirs in operation, but with the town expanding so quickly there was a constant need for more water and it was not until the twentieth century, when the Corporation built the giant Angram and Scar House reservoirs in Nidderdale, over 40 miles from Bradford, that the problem of water shortage was finally solved. Droughts, such as that of 1858, would now be a thing of the past.

The year after the 1858 drought the whole of the centre of Bradford experienced a quite devastating flood, caused by four hours of torrential rain. The nineteenth-century historian John James described the storm as: 'the most dreadful ever witnessed here. Rain fell in torrents, intermixed with large hailstones. The streets were rapidly inundated, as the beck, owing to its contraction by injudicious building on its sides, and over it, overflowed. The lower parts of the town were completely flooded, perhaps to an extent never before known.' The description of the storm and the subsequent flood bears an uncanny resemblance to a similar occurrence a century later, when in the summer of 1968 a violent storm left the centre of Bradford once more under water.

It was estimated that the cost of the damage caused by the 1859 flood amounted to more than £30,000. Even the most tight-fisted councillors realised that the Corporation had to build a better sewerage system than the current one, which simply relied on everything being dumped in Bradford

Beck. Progress was slow, however, and by 1870 only 30 miles of sewage pipes had been laid beneath the main roads. By 1901 scarcely more than a quarter of Bradford houses had water closets and not all of these were connected to the main sewers. The majority of houses still relied on the earth-closet privy, normally shared by several neighbouring families and emptied, it is said, just twice a year. Little wonder that diseases such as cholera persisted.

Bradford Beck flowed into the River Aire at Shipley. William Stansfield, who owned the Esholt estate, complained to the Corporation that the Aire, which flowed across his land, was badly polluted by effluent coming from Bradford. The Corporation responded by purchasing Stansfield's estate in 1906, after several years of wrangling. Bradford's first effective sewage treatment plant was then built at Esholt, the existing plant at Frizinghall being deemed inadequate for the town's needs. In the 1920s an enormous sewage disposal tunnel, 3 miles long, was built between Frizinghall and Esholt. This tunnel was so wide that the civic party which was to open the new facility in 1924 drove through it in a motor car. It was rumoured that when the dignitaries' car emerged from the tunnel at Esholt someone (presumably a political opponent) was heard to say: 'And here comes the first load of shit.'

The Corporation instigated a refuse collection system in 1887 and subsequently set up possibly the first controlled dry-tipping system in the country at Odsal, about 2 miles from the town centre. In 1933 a large part of the Odsal tip was excavated to enable the construction of Odsal Stadium.

Parks, hospitals, workhouses and cemeteries

As noted in an earlier chapter, Bradford's first public park, Peel Park, was opened in 1853. It was purchased by the Corporation in 1870, by which time plans were afoot for creating several other parks. As a result, over the next few years Lister Park was purchased and Bowling Park and Horton Park were laid out, so that there existed a park in each of the townships that had come together to form the borough of Bradford. These places of recreation became particularly popular after the passing of the Bank Holiday Act in 1871 and the growing practice in the 1890s for Saturday to be a half-day of work. The increase in leisure time for working people led to more of them being involved in sports, either as participants or spectators, whereas in previous times sports had normally been the preserve of the wealthy and leisured classes. Interestingly, bearing in mind the hilly nature of the terrain around Bradford, cycling became popular and at least a dozen clubs had been formed in the town by the mid-1890s. Many women became keen participants and cycling was seen by some as an important aspect of female emancipation.

An infirmary had been built between Westgate and Lumb Lane as early as 1843. Charles Semon, a naturalised British subject, was one of the leading figures in Bradford's German merchant community. He became Bradford's first foreign-born mayor in 1864 and was instrumental in establishing the Fever Hospital, near Leeds Road, and the Eye and Ear Hospital in Hallfield Road, near Manningham Lane. In 1874 he founded a convalescent home in Ilkley (this last became a temporary maternity hospital in the 1940s and was, incidentally, where the author first saw the light of day).

For those who were destitute rather than ill there existed the workhouse, opened in 1851 on the site of what later became St Luke's Hospital in Little Horton Lane. Well into the twentieth century some older inhabitants of Bradford were fearful of being admitted to St Luke's, as they associated it with its earlier role as Bradford's workhouse. Undercliffe Cemetery, established in 1851 and privately owned, was the final resting place of many of Bradford's great and good, although it did provide some areas for the burial of the less wealthy. To supplement Undercliffe the Corporation opened Scholemoor Cemetery at Lidget Green in 1877.

Politics and trade

In 1851 the Great Exhibition was held at Crystal Palace and Bradford's worsted manufacturers were well represented. An observer made the following comment:

> The most remarkable exhibition ... referring to alpaca and mohair goods, or mixtures of these with cotton and silk; the trade in which has sprung up within a comparatively short period and progressed with a rapidity and success unparalleled in the history of manufactures. One town alone, Bradford, has risen from the obscurity of a mere manufacturing village to the position of one of the busiest and wealthiest communities in the country ...

For most of this period local political power rested with a group of Nonconformist Liberals, which was so closely knit that in 1850 nine out of

Hazel Bank. (Courtesy of Bradford Libraries)

Bradford's fourteen aldermen attended the same Congregational chapel in Horton Lane. These men were successful businessmen and some were undoubtedly philanthropic – Henry Brown, for example, who was an outstanding mayor in the late 1850s, left £26,000 to charity. Overall, however, to paraphrase a maxim uttered years later by the head of General Motors in America, there was a belief that what was good for the worsted trade was good for Bradford. And certainly if the worsted trade had not flourished as it did there would not have been the political will to enact the measures that helped move Bradford – in a remarkably short time – towards being recognised as an internationally important city.

Much-needed improvements came thick and fast. In the early 1860s many streets in the town centre were widened and improved; new streets linking Bank Street to Kirkgate and Westgate to Darley Street were created. In 1879 Sunbridge Road was laid out and, further from the centre of the town, improvements were made to Oak Lane, Manningham Lane and Queens Road (then called Bolton Lane). In 1871 the Corporation purchased the gasworks from the Bradford Gaslight Company and in 1881 tram tracks, at a cost of £290 per mile, were laid along Manningham Lane, Leeds Road, Sunbridge Road and

Thornton Road. In 1889 Bradford became the first town in Britain to have a municipal electricity supply.

And there was more. In 1865 the Corporation purchased all the manorial rights pertaining to markets. No longer would there be a cattle market in the streets; instead there would be St James's wholesale market (1868), Kirkgate Market (1872) and Rawson Market (1875). In keeping with the town's growing status a Court of Quarter Sessions was established in 1877. A free library was opened in 1872. It was moved to premises in Darley Street in 1878, where it stayed until relocated in the 1960s.

All of these initiatives and improvements were a result of a period of sustained prosperity based on the worsted trade. The twenty years between 1850 and 1870 marked the high point of Bradford's remarkable commercial success. Trade with France, Belgium, Germany and America increased. The American Civil War (1861-65) boosted trade because the blockade of the southern states meant a shortage of cotton, so cotton-warp mixtures doubled in value and the number of Bradford mills producing this type of worsted cloth increased accordingly.

During the 1870s things began to change as a period of stagnation began to affect Britain's economy. In the textile industry competition from French manufacturers became more intense, especially when French designs and all-wool worsteds became fashionable. Because things had been so good for so long there was some complacency in Bradford and firms were slow to invest in the new machinery that would enable them to maintain their competitive-ness. In addition, in 1874 France introduced a 10 per cent tariff on textile imports and America followed suit with the McKinley Tariff in 1890, which led to the Manningham Mills strike of 1890-91. Countries in the British Empire began to develop their own textile industries and this caused many Bradford firms to concentrate on producing yarns for export to these lands rather than finished pieces.

Bradford's manufacturers adopted just one strategy to remain competitive in these difficult times – cutting labour costs. This meant employing more women, who were paid less than men, introducing piece-rate systems and obliging people to look after more machines than before. The result was that while the manufacturers themselves were often cushioned against the effects of the downturn and Bradford ostensibly remained remarkably prosperous, from the point of view of many mill-workers it had become a low-wage town.

Nevertheless, the civic pride that had accompanied Bradford's rise was main-tained, although the town's political complexion began to change. By the 1880s

Kirkgate Market adorned for the coronation of Edward VII, 1901. (Courtesy of Bradford Libraries)

a Conservative revival was under way. The 1867 Reform Act extended the franchise and many of the new voters, whether they were employed in the mills and
warehouses, or were members of an emerging clerical class, became supporters
of the Conservative Party. There were several reasons for this. First of all there
was an opposition on the part of many to the strong Temperance strain of the
Liberals; there was also a growing – almost jingoistic – enthusiasm for imperial-
ism and, connected with this, there was hostility to Gladstone's Irish policy,
which favoured Home Rule. In 1885 a redistribution of Parliamentary seats
gave Bradford three MPs and by 1895 all three were Conservatives. A new
mouthpiece for local Conservatives, the *Daily Argus*, was founded in 1892.

Bradford continued to grow. In 1881 it was decided that the borough
should be extended and in the following year Heaton, Allerton and Tyersal
became part of Bradford. In the same year a dreadful accident took place. The
255ft chimney at Ripley's Newlands mill, which had been built over old mine
workings, collapsed, killing fifty-four people. Ironically, just a year earlier an
all-encompassing Improvement Act had been passed, giving the Corporation
better powers to regulate building construction. Other parts of the Act gave
the Corporation more powers to improve streets, the town's water supply

and the disposal of sewage. Measures were also now in place to strengthen the regulation of places of public entertainment. This key part of the Act gave the Corporation better powers to suppress Bradford's many disorderly houses. That such places existed, and in such large numbers, may surprise those who consider the Victorian age to be synonymous with stern morality and strait-laced prudery.

The City of Bradford

Bradford became a county borough in 1889 and eight years later, on the fiftieth anniversary of its incorporation, Queen Victoria conferred city status on the town. Becoming a city was in some ways a symbol rather than anything else and it was duly accompanied by symbolic features. From 1907 onwards, for example, Bradford's leading citizen would be the lord mayor, rather than merely the mayor. Symbols are important and city status was particularly so, for it marked Bradford's quite remarkable progress from a town that fifty years earlier had been chaotic, unregulated – perhaps even ungovernable – to a modern city. Bradford was now able to take its place among the other great cities of the North, such as Sheffield, Manchester and Leeds, places that had been responsible, through their entrepreneurialism and industry, for making Victorian Britain the most prosperous and influential country in the world.

This is not to say that severe problems no longer existed. The Riot Act had to be read in Bradford town centre at the climax of the bitter Manningham Mills Strike just six years before city status was achieved. And though only the most perceptive could see it, the worsted trade was beginning a slow decline from which it would

Bradford Commercial Bank, Hustlergate, 1877. (Courtesy of Bradford Libraries)

not recover. Poverty and poor housing were still crucial issues, yet it is clear from the large number of terrace houses built in the suburbs from the 1880s onwards – far superior to the back-to-back slum dwellings – that an increasing number of people could afford to rent better housing away from the centre of the city and in a healthier environment. More distant communities became part of Bradford: Idle, Eccleshill, North Bierley, Thornton, Tong and Wyke in 1897. The city's outskirts and suburbs were made more accessible by a growing railway and tram network. After 1911 trolleybuses were introduced. Not to be outdone by the Great Exhibition of 1851, Bradford held its own Bradford Exhibition in Lister Park in 1904. Somewhere in the region of 2½ million people visited the exhibition which was opened by the Prince and Princess of Wales who, on the same visit, unveiled a statue of the recently deceased Queen Victoria in the city centre. Although the city's strong Nonconformist tradition continued a Diocese of Bradford was created in 1919. Bradford now had a Church of England bishop and the parish church became Bradford Cathedral.

While they might be criticised for having some major conflicts of interests, the textile magnates who formed Bradford's ruling elite managed to make some much-needed improvements to the town in the second half of the nineteenth century, despite being faced by a catalogue of daunting challenges. Whether their achievements were a result of enlightened self-interest, altruism, a sense of public duty or a mixture of all these is in some ways irrelevant. What mattered to these hard-headed businessmen was getting things done – and getting their own way. In the next chapter we will look more closely at some of the men who helped to shape Bradford at this time.

seven

THE TEXTILE BARONS

On high ground just over a mile to the north-west of the centre of Bradford stands Manningham Mills, also known as Lister's Mill. This imposing edifice, which from a distance could be mistaken for a gigantic fortress, has dominated the skyline since its completion in 1873, when it replaced an earlier worsted mill that had burned down. The new mill complex, with its floor area of 16 acres, was built in a quasi-Italianate style much favoured by Bradford's commercial and political leaders of the time; the design of its chimney – 249ft high – was based upon the campanile of St Mark's in Venice. Manningham Mills was the largest silk factory in the world and is a breathtaking statement of Victorian self-confidence and enterprise. It was built by Samuel Cunliffe Lister (1815-1906) and helped to make him a multi-millionaire.

Samuel Cunliffe Lister

Samuel was the fourth son of Ellis Lister, who was one of Bradford's first Members of Parliament, elected after the 1832 Reform Act. Ellis was one of the early textile manufacturers in Bradford, building Red Beck Mill in Shipley in 1815, Bank Top Mill in the Horton area in 1817, Bowling Lane Mills in 1819 and Britannia Mills in 1837. In partnership with James Ambler he built the first Manningham Mills, also in 1837. About this time Samuel, who had originally intended to enter the Church, took over his father's enterprises in Bradford and expanded them, but he was more than a business tycoon; he was also an inventor. His first patent, in 1845, was for the Lister Nip Comb which separated and straightened raw wool, a process that previously had to be done by hand and was tediously slow. The Nip Comb revolutionised the textile industry and, because he held the patent, it made Lister rich.

Old Manningham Mills, nineteenth-century drawing. (Courtesy of Bradford Libraries)

But more was to come. In 1855 he began to develop ways of using the fibre found in silk waste, and although he almost bankrupted himself in the attempt he finally perfected a silk-combing machine and a silk-spinning machine, which enabled the production of good-quality yarn at a low cost. Soon afterwards Lister perfected his velvet loom and this ensured him a vast fortune. The velvet produced at Manningham Mills was exported all over the world for more than 100 years, until production finally ceased in the 1990s. In the post-industrial era of the early twenty-first century Manningham Mills underwent a transformation. The outer walls of the main building were retained, but the interior was totally revamped to create a group of modern apartments called Lister Mill.

Lister was not a philanthropist in the manner of some other Bradford textile barons, such as Titus Salt (of whom more later). If anything he was rather disdainful of his workers, especially during the bitter Manningham Mills strike of 1890-91, which will be discussed in detail in Chapter Eight. As a hard-headed businessman, when his wealth enabled him to move to a stately home in North Yorkshire, he sold his Manningham estate to Bradford Corporation in 1870 for it to be used as a public park, stipulating that it be named Lister Park in his honour. Other millionaires might have been more generous and chosen to donate the land to the people of Bradford; Lister could certainly have afforded to make such a gesture. However, thirty years later he did provide £47,500 to build an art gallery and museum in the park. This was the Cartwright Memorial Hall, named, at Lister's behest, in memory of the inventor of the power loom,

Edmund Cartwright (1743-1823). Lister and many other Bradford textile magnates had good reason to be grateful to Cartwright; his invention had made them very wealthy men

The legacy of Bradford's industrial past can be seen throughout the city. Many nineteenth-century buildings associated with the textile trade still exist in the early twenty-first century, some empty and semi-derelict, others being put to new uses. They were built by men who became rich when Bradford was a boom town. Lister, Salt, Ira Ickringill (1836-1911), Isaac Holden (1807-97) Alfred Illingworth (1827-1907) and others like them turned Bradford into a world centre for the manufacture and trading of textiles, especially worsted cloth. Besides running Bradford's industry and trade, these men also dominated the town's political scene; in some cases they became Members of Parliament and made significant contributions to national life. W.E. Forster, for example, was responsible in 1870 for the passing of the Elementary Education Act, which established compulsory education in England.

What sort of men were these Bradford textile barons? They were from a variety of backgrounds and were not always originally from the Bradford area. Indeed some, such as Jacob Behrens, Jacob Moser and Charles Semon, came originally from Germany (see Chapter Five) to make their fortunes in Bradford. James Drummond was from Northumberland and W.E. Forster was born in Dorset. Like Isaac Holden, Reuben Bramhall was from a humble background and started work as a nine-year-old in the coal mines near Wyke, a few miles to the south of Bradford. Abraham Peel's father was a miner and his mother a weaver. Peel himself started work in a mill at the age of seven. At the other end of the social spectrum Lister was born into a wealthy mill-owning family which lived at Calverley Hall and the powerful Butterfield dynasty of Keighley resided in some splendour at Cliffe Castle, which later became that town's museum.

Liberal dissenters

One thing to note is that, until the political landscape began to change in the final decades of the nineteenth century, most of the textile magnates were Liberals rather than Conservatives and Nonconformists rather than members of the Church of England (though Lister was a notable exception to this). In spite of their wealth and power, these men were in their own way following

Bradford's long tradition of dissent from England's upper-class political and religious establishment. In their religious proclivities they mirrored Bradford's population as a whole. The religious census of 1851 showed that, of those who attended church in Bradford, nearly two-thirds were Protestant dissenters. The majority of these (40 per cent) were Methodists, though the Baptists and the Congregationalists (together about a quarter of the total) tended to be more politically active in the town. A minority – fewer than a quarter of churchgoers – were Anglicans. The Catholics, almost all of whom by this time were Irish immigrants, were the only other group of any size, at 9 per cent.

The Tories living in Bradford were usually scathing of this new breed of men who were now in the ascendant in the town. They regarded them as lacking in breeding, and they despised their Nonconformist religion. As early as 1825 John Simpson, a Bradford medical practitioner and a Tory, gave his views about the new elite of Bradford:

> The lower order of people are little removed above the brute creation, being the rudest and most vulgar people under the sun ... A great majority of the richer class is not much better, for they have generally risen from low origin and retain for the most part their vulgar manners. It is a common remark that few know who their grandfathers were, that is, they were in such a low station in life they don't wish to remember them ... Bradford is a great place for dissenters of every denomination ... with the exception of the Unitarians and Roman Catholics, I think the great body of Dissenters in general are a disputatious, ignorant, lowlived set of people ... I never unite good breeding and liberality with either Methodists, Baptists or Independents [i.e. Congregationalists].

That may have been how the Tories viewed them, but the Liberal textile manufacturers themselves naturally had a different opinion. When it came to choosing an editor for the newly-founded *Bradford Observer* in 1833, Benjamin Godwin wrote: '[A newspaper] is about to be established in the hands and under the management of dissenters ... An editor must be a man of high talent and information – of Liberal and reforming principles ... who has just views of religious freedom and the alliance of Church and State ... it is important that the press should be under such guidance.'

Being dissenters, the Bradford industrialists were well aware that they had an affinity with the Puritans of the seventeenth century. The *Bradford Observer*, as can be seen from Godwin's words, was essentially the mouthpiece of the

Liberals in Bradford, and was eventually owned by a triumvirate of Liberal textile magnates, James Hill, William Whitehead and James Roberts. The paper paid Richard Cobden, the champion of free trade, the greatest compliment it could muster when in 1849 it compared him to Oliver Cromwell, 'the incarnate genius of genuine Saxon liberty'. It is no accident that Cromwell's statue features prominently among the stone effigies of the kings and queens of England adorning the façade of the Town Hall, which was built in 1873 when the Liberals were still at the height of their power in the town. It is even possible that some of them would have dispensed with the statues of roy-

Statue of Lister in Lister Park. (Sue Naylor)

alty altogether and just retained that of Cromwell on the front of the building. And eleven years earlier leading Liberal dissenters had organised a series of events to commemorate the bicentenary of the time when 2,000 or so Puritan vicars, including the then Vicar of Bradford, Jonas Waterhouse, had been removed from their livings in 1662, shortly after the Commonwealth had been swept away and the monarchy restored.

Throughout the nineteenth century these Bradford Liberals were in the vanguard of several national campaigns for the removal of statutes and practices that they believed discriminated against Nonconformists. Until 1867 Church Rates (the equivalent of the traditional tithes) were levied, irrespective of whether a person was a member of the Church of England or not. In practice Church Rates were hardly ever collected in Bradford because the Nonconformist majority in the town refused to pay them. Their abolition was hailed as a victory by Bradford's Liberals. In economic matters the Liberals favoured free trade and what nowadays would be called deregulation. They believed – as had their Puritan predecessors – that they should be left alone to run their own lives and business affairs without interference from the government. Understandably they extended this philosophy to the spheres of religion and education. For example, they objected to certain clauses in the Factory Education Bill of 1843, which sought to establish educational facilities for children working in mills and factories. The Liberals believed that any educational provision within the workplace should be done on a voluntary rather than a compulsory basis. They were particularly opposed to the bill's proposal that this provision was to be under the control of the Church of England. Faced with mounting opposition the bill was withdrawn. The Liberals also campaigned for Nonconformists to be allowed full membership of the universities of Oxford and Cambridge, something that was eventually achieved in 1871.

For the Bradford Liberals religious observance was incompatible with any kind of financial support from the public purse. They believed that churches, like individuals, should be governed by the principle of self-help. Consequently they were incensed by the increase in 1845 of the Maynooth Grant, which directed government funds to the Catholic Maynooth College in Dublin. The reality was that the Maynooth Grant was not a sop to Catholicism but a political expedient, intended to enlist the support of the Irish Catholic priesthood in defusing anti-British agitation in Ireland. This rationale clearly cut no ice with Bradford's Liberal elite. Because of their latter-day Puritan sympathies, many of them would also no doubt have had their anger over the Maynooth issue fed by a long tradition of anti-Catholicism, though Titus Salt, for one, never supported the fiercely anti-Catholic Bradford Protestant Association, an organisation not dissimilar to Northern Ireland's Orange Order.

At the heart of the Liberals' various campaigns was a wish to see the disestablishment of the Church of England and an end to its special privileges. Alfred Illingworth in particular argued that the Church of England was really nothing more than an agent of the aristocracy, so disestablishment would reduce the power of the landed gentry and enable the new class of industrialists (such as himself) to take control of the nation's affairs.

Illingworth was the owner of the largest spinning mill in Bradford, Whetley Mills, and related by marriage to the Holdens, who owned Alston Works on Thornton Road and various textile concerns in France. Isaac Holden was Keighley's MP at the same time as Illingworth was a Bradford MP, from 1880 to 1895. Illingworth was a genuine radical. As well as campaigning for religious equality, he supported such things as free non-sectarian education, the extension of the franchise, voting by secret ballot and reform of the laws governing land and property. Fearing that it would compromise his political independence he turned down Gladstone's offer of a seat in the Cabinet.

One problem with the Liberals' concepts of self-help and 'voluntaryism' – a term they coined at the time – was that it could not guarantee any kind of uniformity of provision (critics of Prime Minister David Cameron's 'Big Society' argued this after his policy was launched in 2010). A spinner or weaver at Salts Mill and living in Saltaire in 1872 would have a much better quality of life than someone doing very similar work at, say, Lister's Mill and living in a badly built back-to-back house in a poor area of Manningham. Everything depended on the level of altruism – or rather benevolent paternalism – displayed by the mill-owner. In 1852 Henry Forbes, a former Mayor of Bradford, wrote: 'I say not that there are no grasping masters – men ignorant or regardless of their high moral obligations – but I do say that these men are the exception not the rule: that we have among us many noble "Captains of Industry" between whom and their workmen is some other connection than mere money payment, who study to promote their welfare and elevation ...'

Titus Salt

Titus Salt (1803-76) is the obvious exemplar of Forbes's noble Captain of Industry. Salt's father Daniel had set up a wool stapling business in 1822. It was situated near to Thornton Road in Bradford's Goit Side, which was a particularly overcrowded area, notable for the poverty and ill-health of its inhabitants, so the young Titus would have observed at close quarters the multiple deprivation suffered by his father's workers. Titus took over the business in 1833 and expanded it, developing a particular interest in working with new materials, such as alpaca and Donskoi wool, a particularly coarse wool from Russia, previously thought to be unsuitable for spinning. Even before he built Saltaire, Salt had a reputation as a benevolent employer. In 1847 the *Bradford Observer* praised him in the following way: 'Titus Salt has long enjoyed widespread and well merited popularity throughout this district. His kindness and consideration as an extensive employer, and his munificence and public spirit as an influential citizen has long ago won for him the golden opinion from all sorts of men.'

Salt was elected Mayor of Bradford in 1848, the year after the town became incorporated. This was a difficult year for Bradford's textile trade because the upheavals in France and other parts of Europe severely disrupted the export market. At one point sales from Salt's mills fell by £10,000 a month. Despite this, Salt felt able to offer work to 100 unemployed woolcombers and when trade picked up at the end of the year he gave 2,000 of his workers a day out

at Malham in the Yorkshire Dales, making use of the newly extended railway for the excursion.

Another problem that Salt had to contend with during his year of office as mayor was a cholera outbreak, which claimed more than 400 lives. This outbreak, largely confined to the unsanitary and overcrowded areas of Bradford inhabited by the lower classes, had a salutary effect on those textile magnates, like Salt, who were possessed of a social conscience. The *Bradford Observer* articulated their feelings: 'The cholera most forcibly teaches us our mutual connection. Nothing shows us more powerfully the duty of look-

Statue of Salt in Lister Park. (Sue Naylor)

ing every man upon the needs of another. Cholera is God's voice to his people; as professedly a Christian people we ought not to let so solemn a lesson pass unimproved.' Salt took this message to heart and, as mayor, instigated his own inquiry into the moral state of Bradford. As a magistrate he had seen the effects of poverty and squalor at first hand: '[I have] been confronted with the painful disclosures too frequently made of immorality and vice prevalent among a large class of the population ... [What is] needed is additional efforts to repress profligacy and promote the morality of the town ...' When Salt's report was published in 1850 it recommended better housing, public parks and facilities for education. The *Bradford Observer* supported his demand for better housing:

Let the poor be extricated from the dark damp noisome courts and closes ... suffer them to obtain a view of the sky from their dwellings ... supply them plenty of wholesome water for drinking and purposes of cleanliness ... afford them facilities for the speedy removal of ashes, garbage and all offensive matter. Home will then be sweet home and when the working man leaves his fireside for a walk in the park or an hour in the library or the music hall he will enjoy those advantages more ... because he possesses a house and not a hovel.

Bradford existed under a pall of thick smoke belching from scores of mill chimneys. Salt tried to get the town council to undertake some form of smoke control, but to no avail; his proposal was dismissed as being too expensive. It was really not until the 1956 Clean Air Act came into force that there was any real progress in tackling this problem of air pollution and thick smog was still a frequent problem in the winter months in Bradford right up to the early 1960s. Until that time any visitor to the centre of the city would have been forgiven for thinking that all the public buildings, grand and imposing though they might be, were made out of coal, such was the sooty condition of the stonework. It came as a revelation to many citizens to discover, when the buildings were eventually cleaned, that most of them had been constructed with attractive honey-coloured local stone.

Salt's answer to the problems of pollution, poor housing and a generally unhealthy environment was to take the bold step of relocating his entire enterprise. There were also sound business reasons for the move. If his enterprise was to continue to thrive he really needed to get all his operations under one roof. Some processes – particularly wool combing – were still carried on by outworkers. If he were to make best use of the new wool-combing machines, developed by Lister, Salt would have to bring the outworkers in-house and that meant building a new mill. To build it near to the centre of Bradford on the scale that he envisaged would be too expensive. A site next to the River Aire would be better, as it would guarantee a plentiful supply of water to create the necessary steam-power. Out of a combination of the humanitarian and the commercial, the building of a new community – in fact a new kind of community – was undertaken. Salt hired Lockwood and Mawson to be the architects and gave them this brief: 'To use every precaution to prevent the pollution of the air by smoke, or the water by want of sewerage, or other impurity ... nothing should be spared to render the dwellings of the operatives a pattern to the country.'

Saltaire is about 3 miles north of the centre of Bradford and little more than a mile from Lister's impressive citadel at Manningham. This model suburban village was built in stages by Salt between 1853 and 1876 to house his workers and their families in surroundings that he believed would be conducive to health, temperance and self-improvement. Salts Mill, with 10 acres of floor space, was the largest textile mill in Europe when it was built in 1853. Unlike most other Bradford mills of the time the whole production process, from receiving raw fleeces to producing finished cloth, was carried out on the same premises, hence the complex's huge size. It was more usual for a firm

to specialise in one or perhaps two processes – combing, spinning, weaving, and so on – before passing their cloth on to other firms to carry out the next stages.

Rather than making worsted cloth from sheep's wool, Salt made use of a domesticated breed of llama from South America called the alpaca, which is related to the camel and has a particularly fine silky hair. Especially when it was blended with cotton, alpaca produced a soft, lustrous fabric that was soon in great demand. Using resources other than sheep's wool was not uncommon in Bradford. J.B. Priestley remarked in *English Journey* some eighty years later: 'Indeed, there is nothing that can be spun and woven that does not come to Bradford. I remember myself,

Salt's mausoleum. (Sue Naylor)

as a boy, seeing there some samples of human hair that had been sent from China: they were pigtails which had been cut off by Imperial command.'

When his new mill was opened at Saltaire in 1853 Salt celebrated this – and his fiftieth birthday – by giving a banquet for 3,500 of his workers, brought from the centre of Bradford by train. They dined in the mill's combing shed. The *Illustrated London News* reported the event: 'The opening of the stupendous model mill of Mr Titus Salt, alpaca manufacturer, near Bradford in Yorkshire, was commemorated on the 20th ultimo by a festival on a vast scale – perhaps the largest dinner party ever set down at one time. Mr Salt is one of the most eminent of the Bradford worsted manufacturers ...'

Although it would take another twenty years before Saltaire was completed, it was clear from the outset that Salt had performed a masterstroke by moving his enterprise from the centre of Bradford. The location of the mill in the Aire valley meant better access to road, canal and railway than before, but it was the provision for Salt's workers and their families that grabbed people's attention. The *Illustrated London News* commented on the plans for the model community: 'Every improvement that modern art and science have brought to light has to be put in requisition in the erection of the model town of Saltaire. Healthy dwellings and gardens in wide streets and capacious squares – ample ground for recreation, a large dining hall and kitchens, baths and wash houses, schools, a mechanics institution; these are some of the characteristics of the future town of Saltaire.'

When it was completed in the 1870s, Saltaire occupied 49 acres in total. The mill itself was on a huge scale. The weaving shed contained 1,200 looms, which at full capacity could produce 30,000yds of cloth per day. Workers had houses that were far superior to those they had previously lived in. The community had every facility, including a library, schools and a choice of three churches, one for the Wesleyan Methodists, one for the Primitive Methodists and one – rather grander than the others – for the Congregationalists, Salt's own denomination. When he died Salt was laid to rest in the mausoleum on the south side of this church. The only things missing in Saltaire – and this was deliberate – were public houses and beer shops. Like many of his Nonconformist contemporaries Salt was a keen adherent of the Temperance Movement. Any worker who was found to be the worse for drink was liable to be dismissed from his employment and would therefore probably lose his home as well.

As Salt had expected, his model town became famous and its concept was copied in one way or another by several other paternalistic employers. The Cadburys built Bournville, near Birmingham, to house those who worked at their chocolate factory; and Lever built Port Sunlight, near Liverpool, for the employees of his soap factory.

Salts Mill stopped operating as a textile concern in 1986 and was under threat of demolition for a time. Because of the foresight of a Bradford-born

Salts Mill today. (Sue Naylor)

entrepreneur, Jonathan Silver, that did not happen. Instead the mill was rejuvenated, but rather than producing fine worsteds from alpaca hair it became home to an IT company and an art gallery containing a collection of works by David Hockney. Soon there were boutiques, antique shops and restaurants located within the mill and along the nearby streets. The houses that Salt had built for his workers became fashionable places in which to live and in the early twenty-first century Saltaire became a UNESCO World Heritage Site. But despite being gentrified, refashioned and embraced by the heritage industry, the legacy of Salt remains palpably present in the place he created.

Paternalism and succession

It is easy to forget what a new phenomenon large-scale industrialisation was in the nineteenth century and how quickly people's ways of life were forced to change in the new industrial heartlands. If Lister and Salt had lived a century earlier they might well have been gentlemen farmers or rural squires (which Lister more or less reverted to in his later years). The relationship between the landowner and the farm labourer was established and known, because it had essentially been the same for centuries. But the phenomenal growth of industrial towns and cities within which men, women – and children – were herded together to work in mills and factories, altered everything. In particular, it altered the relationship between employer and employee. A farm labourer in rural England doffed his cap in the belief that the squire not only employed him but was, by some kind of divine law, his social superior and, in a sense, his guardian. How, in a newly industrialised town, was an employee supposed to relate to a mill-owner who, in some cases, might have been a coal-miner or a labourer just a few years earlier? And, conversely, how was the mill-owner – whether self-made man or from an established wealthy family – going to relate to his workforce in this new world of mills and machines? This issue of the relationship between capital and labour exercised men's minds throughout the nineteenth century and gave rise to numerous influential essays and books by people as diverse in their views as Charles Kingsley, Dickens, Andrew Carnegie, Samuel Smiles and Karl Marx.

Paternalism was often the way in which many of Bradford's textile magnates sought to address this issue. None of them would carry the concept as far as Salt and create an entire community based on benevolent paternalism – few, if any, could afford to do so on that scale – but in lesser ways they often adhered to the principles that were writ large at Saltaire. For example, as early as 1835 John Foster built Black Dyke Mills in Queensbury and by the middle of the century he had built about 400 cottages for his employees. He also provided them with a library, an institute, baths and a Sunday school. Some of what he provided can still be seen in Queensbury at the start of the twenty-first century.

In 1834 Henry William Ripley (1814-82) took over the family's Bowling Dyeworks, which he expanded and improved, in particular pioneering the use of chemical dyes. He built a small model community close to his dyeworks and called it Ripleyville. In addition to houses, he provided schools and a church. Ripleyville as such no longer exists, although Ripley Street and Ripley Road remain. Ripley was MP for Bradford between 1874 and 1880, having been previously unseated in 1869 when his opponents lodged an objection under the new Bribery Act. It transpired that Ripley had spent £7,000 (more than twice the combined amount spent by his two opponents) in election expenses and opened 158 rooms supplying free food and drink to voters. Although he started his political career as a Liberal, he later became a Conservative and in 1880 was made a baronet with a seat in the House of Lords.

Isaac Holden's father-in-law, Jonas Sugden, a fervent Methodist, presided over a regime that was scarcely benevolent, though he was motivated by a strong desire to improve the morals of his workers, not so much to save their souls but rather to make them more productive and compliant. His employees were required to attend church and their children were expected to attend Sunday school. Any worker caught gambling or frequenting a public house was liable to be sacked from Sugden's employment.

John Wood (1793-1871) was possibly the earliest of the paternalistic textile manufacturers. He grew up as Bradford's worsted industry was beginning its rapid expansion and became apprenticed to Richard Smith, then owner of the largest spinning firm in Bradford. At the age of nineteen, now qualified as a master spinner, he opened his first mill, bought for him by his father, who was a successful manufacturer of ivory and horn products. Wood provided facilities for woolcombers to work in his mill rather than at home, and in 1825 he built houses for 500 workers. By 1830 he had the largest spinning concern in Bradford with 3,000 employees. He built himself a reputation as a humane employer and donated £40,000 – a huge amount at that time – to support Oastler's Ten Hour Bill, having voluntarily reduced the working hours in his own mills before any reduction became compulsory.

Lister's Mill today. (Sue Naylor)

In the absence of legislation to regulate conditions, voluntaryism (as practised by Wood) and benevolent paternalism (as practised by Salt and some others) were the only ameliorating factors for workers in Bradford's mills. Paternalism was of course more complex than simple altruism; it made commercial sense too. Salt realised that a healthy, sober, reasonably educated workforce was good for business. Ahead of his time, perhaps, he had understood that an enterprise's most valuable asset was its employees, who should be treated as human beings rather than merely as 'hands', as was the case in less enlightened workplaces. The entire Saltaire project could in fact be seen as a shrewd business investment.

The major problem with benevolent paternalism, however, is that it tends to work best when an enterprise is thriving. If there is a decline in trade and the enterprise becomes less profitable, then it will probably be difficult to sustain. We have seen how Salt had generously taken on unemployed men in 1848 even though trade was bad, but that downturn only lasted a year and when the European upheavals subsided the export market for textiles recovered. A more prolonged period of recession could have put an intolerable strain on Salt's generosity. After Salt's death recession resulted in the workforce being reduced at Saltaire from 4,000 to 3,000, and most of those still employed were on short-time as profits dwindled.

Another factor to be considered is that of succession. Salt was not only a benevolent employer and a charismatic personality, but like Lister he was also one of the most able businessmen of his generation. His was a difficult act to follow. Despite the best efforts of his sons and daughters, the firm began to encounter problems in the 1880s, partly because of changes in fashion, partly because of the protectionist policies initiated by America, but also – crucially – because Salt himself was no longer at the helm. In 1892 the business went into liquidation. Although it was rescued by a consortium of Bradford manufacturers and had something of a revival in the twentieth century, it was not possible to sustain the model community in the way Salt had envisaged The whole village was sold off in the early 1930s and the link between the mill company and Saltaire came to an end.

The issue of succession also affected other textile businesses. As was to be expected, the textile barons usually wanted members of their immediate family (normally their sons) to take over when they retired or died. In some cases this worked well, but often the successors, perhaps understandably, did not have the same kind of energetic spirit of innovation and risk-taking as the original textile magnates. Some were sent away to be educated at the major public schools or abroad and thus they developed interests and lifestyles far removed from the single-mindedness that had driven their fathers to make their fortunes in Bradford. As has already been noted in an earlier chapter, Frederick Delius was most reluctant to join his father's textile business and left Bradford as soon as he could. Others, less well-known, no doubt did the same.

eight

STRIKES, UNREST AND
A NEW POLITICAL PARTY

As we have seen in the previous chapter some men made vast fortunes in nineteenth-century Bradford, but for every Salt, Lister and Illingworth there existed in the town many hundreds of families living in extreme poverty. Here is a description by Cudworth from his *Condition of the Industrial Classes* of a typical handloom weaver's diet in the 1840s: 'Malt, treacle and bacon constituted the staple of his diet. Meat he rarely partook of, a bit on Sunday being all that was looked forward to. On that day pieces of fat were put into an iron dish, with potatoes and onions, and after being baked all together without crust were placed on the table in a dish and the family helped themselves from it. For breakfast and supper porridge and milk formed the usual fare.'

This description of an 1840s cellar dwelling, where the very poorest families lived, was printed at the time in the *Morning Chronicle*:

> The scene was perfectly savage ... the floor of earth covered with splints of wood from matchmaking ... a rough wooden tressle [*sic*] on which were placed a broken plate and some herring bones, and a small square box, like a small coffin in which lay an infant. A woman with a skin so foul that she might have passed as a negress was squatted on the ground and a litter, I cannot call them a group, of children burrowed about her ... in one corner lay a bundle of brown rags, the family bed.

The dislocating effects of rapid industrialisation and the huge gap it created between rich and poor meant that periods of tension and strikes were inevitable, particularly in the first part of the century. Between 1850 and 1890 major industrial confrontations were less common, possibly because the textile trade was booming during these years and so work was readily available. Trade unionism in Bradford was never very strong and only made any kind of impact at the time of the 1825 strike and the Manningham Mills strike of 1890-91. For much of the second half of the century many workers appear to have accepted their lot, relying on the paternalism of their employers rather than on trade unions. As historian Patrick Joyce remarks in *Work Society and Politics* (1980): 'the factory towns had dominated not only the physical but the mental landscape of these years to an extent that is now difficult to realise. What a contemporary called "the rule of tall chimneys" had entered into workpeople's lives to a degree that made their

Prosperous people dining at the Midland Hotel, 1890. (Courtesy of Bradford Libraries)

acceptance of the social regime of capitalist industry a matter of inward emotion as much as of outward calculation.'

The 1825 strike

The episodes of conflict and unrest that occurred in Bradford in the first half of the century were almost always a result of the rapid shift towards a factory-based system of textile production. In 1825 a prominent manufacturer, Matthew Thompson, made a rather enigmatic speech in which he seemed to sympathise with the condition of the handloom weavers while simultaneously looking forward eagerly to a greater use of machinery, as he thought that this would somehow be a means of alleviating the problem of unemployment: '[Handloom weavers are] ... suffering such a reduction in wages as to render them totally unable to sufficiently support their families ... Seven years ago ... the general enquiry was, what is to be done with the unemployed population of the country? But, gentlemen, I am happy to say, no such enquiry now exists. Ingenuity and invention are now put to the rack to know how labour can be abridged and what can be done by machinery to supply its place.'

Naturally, the handloom weavers did not share Thompson's optimistic view of the future. They wanted to continue working in their traditional way. In 1824 the Combination Acts were repealed, meaning that people were no longer forbidden from banding together to form trade unions or friendly societies. These Acts had been passed at a time when Britain's political elite was fearful that the spirit of the French Revolution might cross the English Channel. Now the handloom weavers and woolcombers were able to organise themselves into the Combers and Weavers Union, which set about pressing the employers for union recognition and an improvement in pay. The employers responded by attempting to coerce the workers into signing a petition renouncing the union. Those who refused to sign found that their children were dismissed from the spinning mills where they worked. This meant losing an important part of a family's income. A strike started in June 1825 and lasted twenty-three weeks.

People throughout Britain soon became aware of the dispute and £20,000 was raised to support the strikers, but ultimately the strike failed and the weavers and woolcombers were forced to return to work with their pay reduced. But the strike, as is often the case with industrial disputes, was about more than wage rates. It was about the future of the worsted industry; how it would function and develop in an increasingly mechanised environment; how the manufacturers and their employees would relate to each other; and, in particular, where the locus of power would lie and who would derive most benefit from this brave new industrialised world.

Workers leaving Manningham Mills, 1905. (Courtesy of Bradford Libraries)

At the time of the strike the union published a handbill that urged people not to sign the employers' petition. It also summarised what was at the heart of the dispute:

They mean to assail us separately with a request to sign. To sign what? We do not know. Cannot you think or guess? Yes. We think we are to sign away our independence. We think we are to sign away our children's bread. We think we are to sign away our labour at any price which these inhabitants of the higher regions may be pleased to give. This we shall certainly do if we sign against the Union. No sooner shall we have done this then they will ascend to their high abode, laugh at our cowardice and ignorance, bind us to future slavery through our present conduct and we being exposed to [their] ... pride and greediness ... shall be dried and shrivelled up until we are reduced to skin and bone.

After the failure of the strike the manufacturers were able to develop the worsted trade in ways that suited them best, and the workers were forced to

Steam tram at Four Lane Ends, 1882. (Courtesy of Bradford Libraries)

comply. The handloom weavers and woolcombers were still employable for a time, but only as a pool of out-workers for use when required by the employers to complement the mill-based machine operatives. What was particularly attractive to the employers was the ease with which these workers could be dispensed with if trade was slack and re-hired when business improved. Very few employers were like Titus Salt, who was prepared to give work to unemployed woolcombers in 1848 out of a sense of compassion, even though it was a poor year for the industry.

Further unrest

In fact the 1840s as a whole were not good ones for Bradford's poor. In addition to a downturn in trade there was a cholera outbreak in 1848 and the decade also saw the eventual demise of the handloom weavers and domestic woolcombers, now that power looms and Lister's newly-invented combing machines were being used in the mills. In a final attempt to remedy their increasingly desperate situation, those whose livelihood was being destroyed by machines gathered under the umbrella of Chartism. Chartism was essentially a political movement that sought to reform Parliament as a first step in alleviating Britain's economic problems. The Chartists demanded such things as universal male suffrage, payment for MPs and secret ballots. Bradford's handloom weavers and woolcombers, fast becoming an anachronism, were not necessarily interested in these parliamentary reforms. They simply wanted a return to a pre-industrial society where they would have plenty of work. So the words of Feargus O'Connor, leader of the Chartists, were particularly appealing: 'Old English times, old English fare, old English holidays and old English justice, and every man lived by the sweat of his brow ... when the weaver worked at his loom and stretched his limbs in his own field, when the laws recognised the poor man's right to an abundance of everything.'

There were three years in which unrest was particularly noticeable in Bradford. In 1840 the Chartists tried to launch an uprising throughout the West Riding, but it came to nothing. Then in 1842 Thomas Drake, a handloom weaver from Thornton led a series of attacks, known as the Plug Plot Riots, against several Bradford mills, his reasoning being thus: 'We must go to the place where the power looms are for they are the greatest evil we have. We must burn them up and pay no respect of person.' Drake's followers sabotaged several boilers and mill dams to prevent the power looms from running, but repairs were soon made and the overall effect of the sabotage campaign was negligible.

What happened in 1848 was more serious. That year marked the zenith of the Chartist movement in England and coincided with uprisings throughout Europe. For a short time the government had a real fear that there might be a Chartist-inspired revolution in Britain. In Bradford Chartists openly drilled in the Manchester Road area of the town and were only finally dispersed by a combination of Bradford's newly-formed police force, armed with cutlasses, and a company of special constables recruited from Bradford's more prosperous classes. A contingent of fully-armed troops was also hastily brought in via the new railway, but was not required. After this Chartism declined rapidly and Bradford's handloom weavers and domestic woolcombers were forced to forego their traditional independence and seek employment in the mills they had loathed for so long. The only other alternatives were starvation or the workhouse.

By 1850 the worst of the economic depression was over and Bradford began a period of renewed expansion and growing prosperity, which lasted for a generation. Things were generally calmer during this time, but in the 1890s soldiers with fixed bayonets were once again called out to restore order on the streets of Bradford.

The Manningham Mills strike

The Manningham Mills strike of 1890-91 is worth examining in some detail. The dispute and its aftermath were of major significance, not just for Bradford but for the future development of politics and industrial relations in Britain as a whole. After the failure of the strike it could be clearly seen that the Liberal Party could no longer – if it ever really had – adequately represent the interests of working people. In a town like Bradford, where the majority of employers had traditionally been Liberals, the old consensus between the paternalistic employer and his generally compliant workforce had by the late nineteenth century begun to look quite threadbare.

As we have seen in an earlier chapter, Samuel Cunliffe Lister had established his vast Manningham Mills in 1873 to produce plush and velvet and as the 1870s and 1880s progressed trade duly expanded. When his new mill opened the *Bradford Observer* was able to describe Lister's enterprise as follows: 'These gigantic business premises ... formed perhaps the most compact as well as the most

extensive industrial establishments in Yorkshire, if not in England.' Lister and Co. was the biggest employer of labour in Bradford at that time. In 1884 over 4,000 men and women were employed at his mill; by 1890 this figure had risen to more than 5,000. Lister himself had become immensely rich and was viewed as one of Bradford's leading citizens. He was not a modest man, as these remarks printed in

Mural depicting the founding of the Independent Labour Party. (Sue Naylor)

the *Bradford Observer* in December 1890 show: 'I am proud to be able to say that if I have enriched myself I have also benefited thousands and done more for the prosperity of the town of Bradford than any other man.' However, the prosperous days were rapidly coming to an end, and in the same month that Lister made his boastful statement to the press his company set about implementing a reduction in wages for 1,100 workers who worked in the plush department. The reductions were due to come into effect on Christmas Eve (so much for the season of goodwill!), and if they were not accepted there would be a lock-out.

Outraged, the workers held a meeting at the local Primitive Methodist schoolrooms and invited two representatives from the West Riding Weavers' and Textile Workers' Association, William Drew and Allen Gee, to come and advise them on how best to proceed. Drew and Gee suggested that the workers set up a Workpeople's Standing Committee to negotiate with the firm's management. A meeting was duly arranged, at which Mr Reixach, the managing director, outlined the reasons for the company's action. The most important factor, said Reixach, was the United States' recent adoption of the McKinley Tariff, intended to protect domestic industry and trade and thus effectively closing the very lucrative American market to firms like Lister and Co. Similar protectionist tariffs were also being threatened by the French, who already had some measures in place to protect their own industry. Furthermore, the German plush and velvet industry had become increasingly competitive and was now actually exporting textile products to Britain. Cutting labour costs was, according to Reixach, the company's only option, especially (and this enraged the workers) as wage rates at Lister and Co. had been, in his words, 'unnaturally high'. There would, therefore, be no compromise.

The workers met again, this time with Ben Turner, a prominent West Riding socialist, in attendance. Turner made the point that a reduction in the company's profits of 5 per cent was all that was needed to solve the problem of costs, whereas the management of Lister and Co. was about to reduce the workers' average wage by 20 per cent. Lister's personal fortune was, according to Turner, in the region of £6 million, whereas his workers earned on average 14s a week. As regards Lister's workers being over-paid, the reality was, said Turner, that workers in Saltaire, Allerton and Huddersfield were all paid higher wages for similar work. Armed with these statistics the workers met Reixach again, but to no avail. The company refused to budge. By the weekend of 20 December over 1,000 workers were on strike.

The strike polarised opinion in the town. As might be expected, the better-off citizens – with some exceptions – tended to support the hard-line stance adopted by the management, whereas the poorer classes favoured the strikers, who immediately made an appeal for help through the columns of the *Bradford Observer*:

> In the face of these low wages we are of the opinion that we should be not only doing an injustice to ourselves but to the whole textile industry in the West Riding of Yorkshire by accepting the proposed reductions. We earnestly appeal to you for help. Help us to fight against this enormous reduction. Our battle may be your battle in the immediate future. We trust, therefore, that in our present state of need and disorganisation you will liberally support us.

Support came quickly, over £100 being raised on the first day of collecting. Letters of sympathy and contributions to the strike fund came from all over Britain and from workers' organisations in France, Germany and America. About £11,000 had been raised by the time the strike ended in April 1891, but it was not enough to sustain the strikers, especially when workers not initially threatened with reduced wages joined the dispute. It was estimated that 5,000 people were on strike by March 1891.

One thing that particularly incensed the strikers and their supporters was a letter which Lister himself wrote to the *Bradford Observer* that winter:

> That they have earned in the past not only good wages but very good wages, is certain, or the Manningham ladies, the 'plushers' as they are called, could not dress in the way they do. Silks and flounces, hats and feathers, no lady in the

town can be finer. No one likes better to see them comfortably and befittingly dressed than I do; but there is reason in all things. But what is the moral of all this? What I never cease to preach and teach – utter want of thrift. The women spend their money on dress and the men in drink; so the begging box goes round – it matters not what their wages are.

The *Bradford Observer* had traditionally been the mouthpiece of Bradford's Liberal establishment and thus a supporter of paternalistic employers. However, the editor, Charles Byles, had sympathy with the strikers – especially as Lister was a Conservative, rather than a Liberal – and he felt moved to rebuke the mill owner for his insensitive remarks: 'But Mr Lister should be well aware that the present is not the most judiciously chosen time for his lecture on thrift ... In Mr Lister's eyes, probably the spending of an extra shilling a week on dress and drink represent the acme of short-sightedness and foolish self-indulgence, and the purchase of the big estates seems the perfection of far-sighted thrift and philanthropy.'

Meanwhile, the avowedly Conservative *Yorkshire Evening Post* adopted a tactic sometimes seen in more recent times when working-class politicians (such as John Prescott) come under attack. Rather than attempting to counter their arguments, it simply mocked the way in which the strikers' leaders spoke: 'What a terrible diction do working man orators sometimes use! There was a meeting of trade unionists and strike sympathisers at Bradford in aid of the Lister strike hands and one leader of labour principles informed his audience in strident tones that he was 'diabolically opposed' to any reductions whatever.'

Throughout January and February 1891, as the number of workers on strike steadily grew, over £1,000 per week was eventually needed to sustain them through what was a particularly hard winter, with heavy snowfalls recorded as late as mid-March. Such a large sum became more and more difficult to find, yet the strikers – certainly for a time – seemed more determined than ever to hold out, despite the obvious hardships many families were experiencing. Bradford's Poor Law Guardians were not sympathetic, and no relief was given to the families of strikers, nor to any unemployed person who refused to work for Lister and Co. Likewise, the Watch Committee and the police appear to have been fully supportive of the employers, as the *Yorkshire Factory Times* commented in February 1891: 'The law with its myriad ways of help is used to the fullest extent in the endeavour to beat the strikers ... Men and women are taken into custody, and run into the front office, for no other purpose than to damage the work-people in the eyes of the management.'

A busy Lister Park, 1914. (Courtesy of Bradford Libraries)

As the weeks passed the strikers demonstrated more vociferously and in greater numbers in the centre of the town, and the strike began to attract attention beyond Bradford. There were large demonstrations of support in Leeds and Halifax. It also became clear that the focus of the dispute was beginning to shift from the specific issue of wage rates at one Bradford mill to a wider issue – the conflict between those with power and money and those who had very little of either. The mouthpiece of the strikers, the *Yorkshire Factory Times*, made the point forcibly in March 1891: 'After the action of the magistrates and others in authority in the past four weeks there can be no possible question that there are undue influences at work against the strikers (who are generally admitted to have a just cause); and that the principle of the struggle affects every worker throughout the length and breadth of the United Kingdom. In other words, the fight is between capital and labour – the classes against the masses.' At the time the strike ended in April 1891 the paper repeated this theme: 'The operatives have from the first been fought not only by their own employers at Manningham but by the whole monied class of Bradford. From the highest dignitary to the lowest corporate official "law and order" has been against them.'

The Watch Committee made an order at the end of February 1891 banning strike meetings in any building in the centre of the town. These meetings had often taken place on a Sunday and three reasons for the ban were given: large crowds assembling outside St George's Hall (the usual venue) on previous Sundays had blocked entrances to the building, thus causing a fire hazard; irreligious and blasphemous remarks had been heard in the hall and these were unacceptable, especially on a Sunday; and Bradford's chief magistrate had been insulted at one of the meetings. After this action by the Watch Committee the focus of the dispute shifted yet again, this time to the issue of freedom of speech and assembly. There was an increase in numbers attending open-air meetings, as these were not yet subject to the ban and so on Easter Monday (30 March) a crowd of more than 20,000 assembled in the centre of Bradford. Although this meeting passed off peacefully, clearly things were coming to a head.

On 12 April permission was grudgingly given by the Watch Committee for a meeting to be held at St George's Hall. Ben Tillett, the nationally known leader of the 1889 London dock strike, had agreed to come to Bradford to address the meeting. Knowing that St George's Hall would be full to capacity, the strike leaders sought permission from the Watch Committee for an additional meeting to be held in nearby Town Hall Square. Permission was refused, but the meeting went ahead anyway. Scuffles broke out in the square between the police and members of the crowd. Two or three of the strike leaders were arrested, but later released without being charged.

On the next day, Monday 13 April, things became much more serious. Throughout the day it became obvious that bands of self-styled anarchists, socialists and communists were arriving in Bradford by train from as far afield as London, as well as from Leeds, Sheffield and Lancashire. By now the conflict had definitely moved well away from a local industrial dispute. Here were groups of avowed revolutionaries from across Britain seeking to challenge the authorities through a direct confrontation on the streets of Bradford. In short, they had come for a fight. What happened next made national news, and the next day *The Times* carried the following report:

the disturbances which commenced yesterday afternoon became serious during the evening, so much so that throughout the whole of the night the town was one scene of disorder and uproar. The military had to be called out and the Riot Act was read by the Mayor ... the military paraded the street and charged the people in various directions ... a baton charge by the police was found necessary ... Open knives were thrown at the police at times. Up to midnight the streets were crowded and the military were making charges with fixed bayonets but the stone-throwing had then ceased.

The disturbances were repeated the following night. Again the mayor was compelled to read the Riot Act and again troops with fixed bayonets were called upon to disperse the crowds. It was a miracle that nobody was killed on these two nights of rioting, although there were some injuries to people and to police horses. Surprisingly few arrests – just ten on the Monday night – were made. The town remained relatively peaceful the rest of the week

An open-air protest meeting was planned for the following Sunday, 19 April. Fearing another riot, the Watch Committee arranged for 300 soldiers to be on hand and Bradford's police force of 200 men was augmented by reinforcements from neighbouring towns. It was estimated that between 60,000 and 90,000 people attended the meeting, which passed a resolution condemning the Watch Committee for infringing the right of free speech and free assembly. The strikers' cause itself was relegated to a supporting role at the meeting, which passed off quite peacefully; the troops and their bayonets were not needed.

Despite this ostensible evidence of widespread support, the reality was that at this point the strike was beginning to crumble through lack of funds, and many families were in dire financial straits. The *Leeds Daily News* described the situation in April 1891 as follows: 'the distress among the workpeople has been very severe. To keep households going all kinds of articles have been freely pawned … there are now lying in the Bradford County Court some 60 warrants of execution to be levied for goods and rent.' Such hardship meant that the dispute could not continue. The silk weavers were the first to give in and by the end of April the strike was over. The employees of Lister and Co. returned to work and to reduced wages.

In terms of a trade dispute the nineteen-week strike was a defeat for the workers, but its significance went far beyond Manningham Mills. In a new world of tariffs and increased competition from foreign manufacturers there could no longer be a guarantee of a steady growth in prosperity for the textile trade, such as had been enjoyed in the 1850s and 1860s. And it was now clear that when the chips were down the old spirit of benevolent paternalism on the part of the employers would no longer apply. Those with power and wealth would stand together to protect what they had. It was time for the workers to reconsider their traditional allegiance to the Liberal Party. It was perhaps time for a new political party.

The Independent Labour Party

George Orwell, the author of *1984* and *Animal Farm*, is probably the most well-known person to have been a member of the Independent Labour Party (the ILP). The ILP sent a group of twenty-five volunteers, including Orwell, to serve with the Republican forces that were fighting against Franco's fascist rebels in the Spanish Civil War of 1936-39. Orwell's experiences in that war are vividly recounted in his classic work, *Homage to Catalonia*.

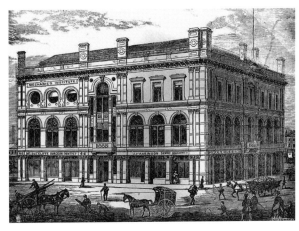

Mechanics Institute sketch 1870. (Courtesy of Bradford Libraries)

The ILP was founded nearly fifty years earlier in Bradford as a direct consequence of the Manningham Mills strike. Today a large commemorative mural, rather similar to the ones normally associated with paramilitary factions in Belfast, can be seen painted on the side of a building towards the bottom of Leeds Road, quite close to the site of Firth's Temperance Hotel, where the Bradford ILP was born in January 1893. The previous year Fred Jowett, who was to be elected as Bradford's first ILP Member of Parliament in 1906, summed up the rationale behind the founding of this new political party: 'In the Lister strike, the people of Bradford saw plainly, as they had never seen before, that whether their rulers are Liberal or Tory they are capitalists first and politicians afterwards.' Charles Glyde, the editor of the *Bradford Observer* and a supporter of the Manningham Mills strikers, spoke in a similar vein: 'We have had two parties in the past – the can'ts and the won'ts and it's time we had a party that will.'

The first chairman of the ILP was Keir Hardie and other notable early members were Philip Snowden and Ramsay MacDonald, who was chairman from 1906 to 1909. MacDonald went on to become the United Kingdom's first Labour Prime Minister later in the twentieth century.

From the start the ILP accommodated a broad spectrum of political opinion. Under its banner were gathered conventional socialists, Scottish nationalists, Marxists, Methodists and Fabian gradualists. The party failed to gain any seats in Parliament in the 1895 general election, and it was really only when it became an affiliate of the newly formed Labour Party in 1906 that it made much electoral headway, though it always provided a good proportion of Labour Party activists in those early years.

In Bradford itself the party, after a shaky start, made good progress, and by 1914 it was polling more than 40 per cent of votes in the local elections, prompting one of its members, J.H. Palin, to state the following at the ILP Conference, held in Bradford that year: 'of ordinary historical associations, Bradford has none. In [the] Domesday book it is described as waste, and subsequent periods of capitalist exploitation have done little to improve it ... The history of Bradford will be very largely the history of the ILP.' While these comments are obviously biased, they do say something about the confidence that the ILP in Bradford was feeling at the time. It had already encouraged the development of educational classes, cultural activities and social clubs – there was even a Labour Cricket League. Now that it had more political power the party embarked upon a programme of improvements in Bradford, in housing, education and public health, more detail of which will be given in a later chapter. Suffice it to say at this stage that this attempt at municipal socialism did not

The Jolly Butchers public house, 1907. (Courtesy of Bradford Libraries)

always go down well with the ILP's supposed allies in the Labour Party. Thus the ILP was attacked by the Marxists for allegedly propping up the capitalist system by initiating these municipal reforms, to which the reply was given that remedying the worst excesses of capitalist society had to be the first priority.

The ILP also lacked support in some parts of Bradford where the populace was predominantly Irish. The Irish immigrants had traditionally been firm supporters of the Liberal Party because of its home rule for Ireland policy. Also, there was Catholic hostility to any party that was even slightly connected with atheistic Marxist groups. Writing in the *Bradford Labour Echo* after the disappointment of the 1895 general election, the ILP activist E.R. Hartley said this about the predominantly Irish slum areas of Bradford's South Ward:

> The South Ward is a Liberal anti-Labour Ward ... It is not from people such as are to be found in this locality that our emancipation will ever come. Socialism is a science of government. It requires intelligent men and women to grapple with its tenets and to look for such among the mass of unfortunate wretches who make up the sum total of wretchedness in the South Ward is to look in vain. The very people for whom we are working and toiling are our worst opponents – bitter and intolerant, unsympathetic and insolent, prone rather to live on charity than upon the rights of manhood and womanhood and if ever such places are captured at all they must be captured from the outside, for not until the death rate, the insanitation and the horrible mode of life are changed shall we ever see the South Ward of Bradford taking an intelligent interest in the affairs mostly concerning it. This is no skit but a sorrowful admission of the plain facts as I see them.

Hartley's description has definite echoes of Cudworth's account of the miserable living conditions endured by the poor in the 1840s. For some sections of Bradford's population not much had changed in the intervening years. It was the desire to do something about the terrible social conditions in the poorer parts of Bradford that motivated the ILP to undertake its programme of reforms once it had achieved more influence on Bradford Council.

The coming of the Great War in 1914 caused some confusion for the ILP. Its official stance was pacifist, but many of its members supported Britain's war effort and joined the armed forces as eagerly as anyone else. After the war the ILP stagnated, even though the Labour Party itself had periods as the government of the day. In 1932 a decision was made to separate from the Labour

Party, but in 1947 the three ILP members who still remained in Parliament rejoined the Labour Party. In 1975 the ILP was finally wound up.

This was a rather downbeat end for the party, but the importance of the ILP does not rest with what happened in its later years but rather with what it achieved before 1914. It was instrumental in breaking the dominance of the Liberal Party, both locally and nationally, and it became the foundation stone of a totally new political force – the Labour Party – which would henceforward attempt to represent the interests of the working-class in a way that the Liberal Party could never really do. Nineteenth-century liberalism championed unfettered free trade and paternalism. While it might contain certain elements of radicalism and humaneness, which would at times benefit the working-class, it was essentially a political philosophy best suited to the needs of the manufacturers and entrepreneurs who controlled industry and trade in places like Bradford. It had taken a century of robust and at times painful development for people to begin to understand how capital and labour would co-exist in an industrial society. The traditional verities of a pre-industrial age had been swept away, never to return. After Archduke Ferdinand was assassinated in Sarajevo in the summer of 1914 many other things would also be swept away, as we shall see in the next chapter.

nine

BRADFORD
AND THE FIRST WORLD WAR

In order to understand fully the twentieth-century history of Bradford, we must start our quest among the rolling, fertile countryside around the River Somme in northern France. About half-way between the city of Arras and the town of Albert lies the village of Hébuterne, an unexceptional collection of houses and farms set among the undulating landscape of the Pas-de-Calais. Near the centre of the village is a church and on the churchyard wall, next to the road, is a small plaque – easily missed, unless one knows it is there. On the plaque, underneath Bradford's coat of arms and the insignia of the West Yorkshire Regiment, is written the following:

IN MEMORY OF
THE BRADFORD PALS
16th AND 18th BATTALIONS WEST YORKSHIRE REGIMENT
THEIR NAME LIVETH FOR EVERMORE

There is a memorial to the Bradford Pals in the centre of Bradford, and in Bradford Cathedral there is a commemorative stained-glass window and a plaque. However, the Hébuterne memorial is the only one that is actually in France itself and therefore in the vicinity of tragic events that were to have a lasting effect upon the fortunes of Bradford.

Just a few miles south of Hébuterne is the Sheffield Memorial Park, established to commemorate those men from towns and cities in the north of England – Hull, Accrington, Barnsley, and so on – who were members of the British Army's 31st Division and who were killed at the Battle of the Somme in the summer and autumn of 1916. The location of the park is precisely where the 31st Division went into action on the first dreadful day of the battle, 1 July 1916.

The two Bradford Pals battalions were part of this division too, but strangely enough there is no memorial to them in the Sheffield Memorial Park. There are plenty of monuments to be seen, some rather imposing ones, such as those commemorating the Barnsley Pals and the Chorley Pals, but nothing for the men from Bradford who fell, except that single, rather plain plaque on a church wall some miles away from where most of them died.

All over by Christmas

As soon as war was declared in early August 1914 there was a rush of volunteers to recruitment centres throughout Britain. In Bradford hundreds turned up at Belle Vue Barracks on Manningham Lane, keen to join the 6th (Territorial) Battalion of the West Yorkshire Regiment. Many were turned away because they failed to pass the medical examination, which tells us something about the poor health of many people in England's industrial cities at that time. Others who were fit enough found that the battalion was already up to full strength, so they were sent home and told to wait. J.B. Priestley, later to become Bradford's most famous writer of the twentieth century, was not prepared to wait. He walked to Halifax and signed up with the Duke of Wellington's Regiment, which had its headquarters in the town. His impatience may have saved his life, for it meant that he was not to be involved in the carnage that would overtake the Bradford Pals on the Somme in 1916, though he was wounded in France, and eventually discharged in 1918 as unfit for active service after being gassed.

What were the authorities going to do about all these eager young men kicking their heels at home? Obviously they would be needed to serve King and Country as soon as possible, but how best to involve them only became clear after Lord Derby made an emotional appeal for volunteers in Liverpool in late August. In his speech he referred to the creation of 'a Battalion of Pals' in Liverpool. This expression was reported in the national press and quickly caught on with the public. Within days many northern cities and towns were beginning to make plans to raise their own local Pals battalions. Bradford was no exception. The First Bradford Pals battalion was raised in the autumn of 1914, to be followed by the Second Bradford Pals the following spring. Officially these formations were designated the 16th and the 18th Battalions of the West Yorkshire Regiment.

At first sight the concept of a Pals battalion might seem quite a good one, for it guaranteed that on volunteering to join the army a man would be with people he already knew; his neighbours, the people he worked with and

played with, or even prayed with – his pals. 'Join together. Serve together' was a very powerful slogan, and the Pals battalions were without doubt an excellent recruiting device, playing on local loyalty and a sense of comradeship and togetherness. The great drawback would only become apparent later in the war, when the industrial scale of the conflict and great military disasters, like the Somme offensive, would mean that whole communities lost many of their menfolk in one go. In Bradford's case hundreds were killed before lunchtime in a single day. After the events of summer 1916 numerous houses throughout Bradford drew their curtains to signify that the families were in mourning.

Stained-glass memorial window in Bradford Cathedral for 6th Battalion, West Yorkshire Regiment. (Sue Naylor)

But nobody could foresee this in September 1914. Many of the young men itching to join up were even anxious that it might be all over before they had a chance to get involved and show their mettle. As ever, when a popular war breaks out, people thought that victory would be achieved by Christmas (and, of course, the Germans thought this too). So the mood within the newly-formed Pals battalions was one of cheery optimism and good fellowship.

Because Belle Vue Barracks was still needed as headquarters for the Territorials and because the nearby Artillery Drill Hall was deemed too small, the First Bradford Pals had as their temporary headquarters a defunct roller-skating rink on Manningham Lane, just a couple of hundred yards from the barracks. Whoever thought of using the Rollerina as the headquarters deserves to be congratulated, for it provided an ideal indoor parade ground for the Pals, with various other rooms that were easily converted into offices and stores. Most recruits viewed the Rollerina as ideal for other less military reasons too. It was handy for the pubs and shops on Manningham Lane. The recruits were able to go home every night, and the comparatively short hours they had to spend on duty each day meant that most enjoyed an easier life than when they had been working in an office or mill. Often the Pals marched up Manningham

Lane to drill and do PT in Manningham Park. And when they got their uniforms in November – navy blue serge of the highest quality, made in Bradford of course – they probably felt ready to chase the Hun out of Belgium and France single-handedly, if called upon.

As with most things in Britain at that time, the organisation of the Pals battalions was often based on class-distinctions. This is perhaps best illustrated by looking at the nicknames of the four Pals battalions from Hull. The first of these, while officially designated the 10th Battalion of the East Yorkshire Regiment, was familiarly known as the Hull Commercials, because most of its recruits were from the managerial and clerical classes of the city. The next battalion was known as the Hull Tradesmen, as it drew on the class of small shopkeepers and the self-employed. Then came the Hull Sportsmen, recruited from members of local football, cricket and rugby clubs. And finally there was the Hull T'others, a battalion whose members, one assumes, might have suffered some feelings of inferiority compared with their peers in the other three units. At least they were not called the Hull Also-rans.

The two battalions of the Bradford Pals were not given nicknames like these, but it is clear that considerations of class were well to the fore from the start of the recruitment process in September 1914. The *Yorkshire Observer* remarked in its edition of 12 September that only 'the right sort of men' should be allowed to join. Recruitment was in the hands of the Executive Committee of the Citizens' Army League, a body made up of Bradford's most influential men. This body even went so far as to propose (according to the *Yorkshire Observer* again) that the eight companies which were to form the First Bradford Pals Battalion should be clearly organised along class lines, with A Company consisting of professional men and employers, B Company of higher-grade office workers, C Company of clerks, D Company of warehousemen, and so on until we come to H Company, which was to be made up of those designated as 'miscellaneous'. While class distinction is certainly still apparent in English society in the twenty-first century, it is not usually as nakedly overt as that shown here, a century ago.

In the event this rigid and rather snobbish approach was dropped, but it is clear from a report published in the *Bradford Weekly Telegraph* in November 1914 that the First Bradford Pals was made up of a disproportionate number of people who later generations would term white-collar workers. Most were clerks, skilled workers, professional men and the self-employed. Unskilled manual workers, by far the most numerous group in Bradford's workforce,

1 Images of Bradford captured in an iron gate sculpture at the bottom of Ivegate.

2 One of Bradford's imposing mosques – Jamiyat Tabligh-ul-Islam Mosque.

3 Bradford University.

4 Manningham Mills, now refurbished as Lister Mill.

5 The New Beehive, Westgate, a traditional Bradford pub, still gas-lit in the twenty-first century.

ABOVE 6 The Harp of Erin, in an area
of Bradford settled by Irish immigrants
in the nineteenth century.

LEFT 7 In Centenary Square protestors
in 2011 follow a long tradition of dissent
in Bradford.

8 Bandstand in Roberts Park, Saltaire. The park, originally called Saltaire Park, was created in 1871 and restored in 2010. Its current name commemorates James Roberts, who was the manager of Salts Mill in the 1920s.

9 Samuel Cunliffe Lister's Manningham Mills dominates Bradford's northern skyline.

10 Eastbrook Hall, built in 1904 as the Methodist Cathedral of the North. After years of dereliction the refurbished building was opened by HRH Prince of Wales in 2008 and now contains seventy-three apartments.

11 An oasis of pre-Industrial Revolution houses at Little Horton Green.

12 Spices for sale.

13 Inside the Wool Exchange, now restored as a branch of Waterstones.

14 The Wool Exchange.

15 Jamil Food Store, a typical corner shop in a predominantly Asian area of Bradford.

On 22nd July 1786
John Wesley
Anglican Minister and
founder of Methodism
preached from this window
on the text   Mark 3v35

16 Now a balti house in Baildon village, once the site of one of John Wesley's many preaching visits to Bradford.

17 On the world-famous Ilkley Moor, near to Cow and Calf Rocks.

18 The Industrial Museum houses textile machinery from Bradford's heyday as 'Worstedopolis'.

19 Titus Salt School at Saltaire, named in honour of one of England's most philanthropic industrialists.

RIGHT 20 The plaque inside Haworth Parish Church indicating where members of the Brontë family are laid to rest.

THE
BRONTË FAMILY
VAULT
IS SITUATED BELOW
THIS PILLAR,
NEAR TO THE PLACE WHERE
THE BRONTËS' PEW STOOD
IN THE OLD CHURCH.
THE FOLLOWING MEMBERS
OF THE FAMILY
WERE BURIED HERE
MARIA AND PATRICK.
MARIA, ELIZABETH,
BRANWELL,
EMILY JANE, CHARLOTTE.

BELOW 21 Lister Park and Cartwright Hall in springtime. The park was originally Lister's estate; Cartwright Hall was purpose-built as Bradford's art gallery and museum.

22 The Black Bull at Haworth, where the luckless Branwell Brontë did much of his drinking.

23 Some former mills and warehouses have been refurbished and put to new uses; others, like these, are still awaiting a new role.

24 New Market Place, with its monument to Bradford's twin cities and towns throughout the world.

25 Students from Bradford's Asian community at work at Belle Vue Girls' School.

ABOVE 26 The Alhambra Theatre, opened in 1914 and extensively refurbished in 1986, seen here at night.

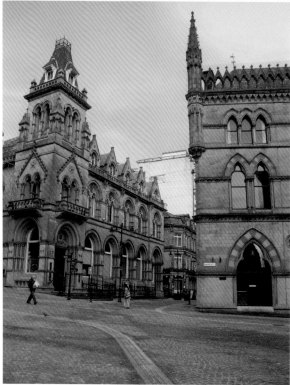

LEFT 27 Hustlergate, named after John Hustler, one of Bradford's pioneering entrepreneurs.

28 Bradford City Hall, built in the 1870s when Bradford was at the height of its commercial power and influence.

LEFT 30 Councillor Naveeda Ikram, England's first woman Muslim Lord Mayor and in office in Bradford 2011-2012. (Courtesy of Bradford Council)

BELOW 31 Bradford City Hall.

according to the 1911 Census, made up little more than a tenth of those recruited that autumn. The *Yorkshire Observer* reported that the recruits were generally taller than the average too. This was shown when they were kitted out with their uniforms. The recruits were taller because in general they came from relatively prosperous backgrounds. Given their occupations, it is also safe to assume that most of the recruits would have been better educated than the average Bradford citizen. In other words, almost by deliberate design the Executive Committee of the Citizens' Army League had managed to ensure that the Pals were comprised of what might be described as the cream of Bradford's young men, the very ones who would have been expected, in due course and given a normal peacetime lifespan, to move into positions of leadership and responsibility, not just within their trades and professions but also within Bradford's civic and community life. While the Citizens' Army League can hardly be blamed for wanting to recruit what it believed to be Bradford's brightest and best, this selection policy was to have a very unfortunate and unintended outcome. If, after the war, local business firms lacked the same drive and talent that had made the city one of the most dynamic and prosperous in all Europe before 1914, surely some part of the reason must lie in the fact that so many of Bradford's most promising young men were killed on the Somme. Then again, some people have expressed the opinion that Britain as a whole has never really recovered from that catastrophic episode.

1 July 1916

The first day of the battle, 1 July 1916, was the worst. Indeed it was the worst day for casualties – 60,000 in total, with 20,000 killed – that the British Army has ever experienced. It was the first time that the two Bradford Pals battalions had been involved in any heavy fighting. They had previously served in Egypt for several months, guarding the Suez Canal against the Turks, but had seen no action, (though the First Pals were once on the receiving end of what today would be called friendly fire, when a Royal Artillery unit mistakenly shot at them). The Pals had been in France since March 1916, and from April onwards they had manned the front line for periods of five days at a time, alternating with ten days behind the lines, resting in billets or in reserve. Both battalions had suffered casualties; two men were killed by artillery fire on Easter Sunday. Other casualties occurred as the weeks went on, but these were within the parameters of what might be expected. The Battle of the Somme was to be of a totally different magnitude.

The Somme offensive was originally intended to relieve some of the pressure that the French were having to endure at Verdun, where for months things had been going so badly that the French commander, General Joffre, had told his British counterpart, Sir Douglas Haig, that unless a British offensive took place the French army would cease to exist by August 1916. In fact, because of concerns about their own mounting casualties, the Germans had actually ceased their attacks against Verdun by early summer. So why then did Haig continue with his Somme strategy? There were two main reasons, the first of which was concerned with issues of diplomacy and the second with issues of military strategy. First, the offensive would give an opportunity for the French and the British armies to fight side by side for the first time, thus showing that the two armies could work together and that the British (who were to commit substantially more troops) were now pulling their weight. And secondly, Haig, discounting the grave reservations expressed by some of his subordinates, firmly believed that here was the very place where a major offensive could lead to eventual victory in the war, although what had led him to this belief has never been made clear. After all, the force at his disposal was largely made up of enthusiastic volunteers, not seasoned professional soldiers – most of them had been killed or incapacitated by this stage of the war. Furthermore, the German forces facing his troops occupied well-established positions, often on higher ground than the British, meaning that the attack would, in many cases, literally be an uphill struggle. Nevertheless, although he knew that the British army was not in a proper state of readiness, with many of the units under his command – including the Bradford Pals – having had very little combat experience, Haig went ahead and launched his offensive.

Both of the Bradford Pals battalions were to take up positions with the other units of the 31st Division near the left flank of the assault line. The division's principal objective was to capture the village of Serre. As was usual with a major offensive, the troops who were to carry out the initial assault did not enter the front line until a comparatively short time before the attack was scheduled to begin. Consequently, in the late afternoon of the day before the attack the men of 93 Brigade, which consisted of the two Bradford battalions, the Durham Pals and the Leeds Pals, were resting a few miles behind the lines in a small village called Bus-les-Artois. They had been given a pep-talk by the corps commander, Sir Aylmer Hunter-Weston, in which he had warned that any man shirking his

Memorial to Bradford Pals in central Bradford. (Sue Naylor)

duty or trying to run away would immediately be shot by the military police. Many of the Pals were incensed by this implication that some of them might be cowards. Also present at a pre-battle briefing had been the commander of the 31st Division, Major-General Robert Wanless O'Gowan, who – on the basis of no evidence whatsoever – blithely informed the troops that the British artillery barrage had killed all the Germans around Serre and so the Pals' task would be an easy one. It goes without saying that neither of these high-ranking officers took part in the assault the next day.

When evening came the battalions started to move towards their front-line positions, from which they would launch the assault the next morning. Although the distance between Bus-les-Artois and the assembly trenches was just a few miles, the confusion caused by the darkness, the congestion in the communication trenches and the deafening artillery barrage meant that the Pals did not reach their jumping-off points until the early hours.

The British artillery barrage had been going on for several days, and was so intense that there were reports that it could be heard as far away as Hampstead Heath. The barrage was by no means as successful as people had predicted, or as the Pals had confidently been assured by the generals, for the Germans had constructed elaborate dug-outs up to 40ft deep in the chalky rock of the Redan Ridge, where their front line was situated, and this had enabled them to survive the week-long onslaught with relatively few casualties. As soon as the barrage lifted on the morning of 1 July the Germans knew for certain that a British infantry attack was imminent, so they were able to scramble out of their subterranean strongholds and position their machine guns to repel the British assault. This they did with great success. Poor planning by the British generals also meant that the 31st Division's left flank was completely exposed. The Germans, realising this, had increased the number of their heavy guns and deployed them to exploit this weakness. When the British attacked they were subjected to devastating artillery fire in addition to machine-gun fire.

Zero hour came at 7:30 a.m.: whistles blew to signal the advance and the Pals climbed out of their trenches. They were mown down in their hundreds, many before they had gone a few yards. The assault on Serre was a complete failure, so much so that at 11 a.m. the commander of 93 Brigade, Brigadier-General John Darnley Ingles, called off the attack, later recording the following in the brigade war diary: 'I could observe none of our troops advancing on right or left and the Germans were holding their front line in strength. Taking into consideration our heavy losses ... and the scarcity of officers and NCOs I decided that a further advance would be fruitless ...' Perhaps Captain Dr.G.B. McTavish, the medical officer of the Second Bradford Pals, best summed up the impact of the disaster in a letter home, now held by the Imperial War Museum: 'I'm sure you don't want to hear much about what I've been seeing lately ... I'll never forget July 1st as long as I live. It was an awful day.'

The casualties suffered by the two battalions of the Bradford Pals were horrendous. Out of a total of 770 men of the First Pals who went into action on that day 515 were reported killed, seriously wounded or missing. Every officer was a casualty. The Second Pals suffered 490 casualties out of 697 who went into action. Many who were wounded later died.

A century later the whole area across the Somme battlefield is dotted with immaculately-tended military cemeteries. The graves of Bradford Pals can be found in some of these, especially in those that are nearest to where the two battalions launched their futile assault that morning. Every cemetery has a register, giving details of who lies where. However, many graves have headstones without names. For example, Euston Road Cemetery, near the village of Colincamps, which was just behind the Bradford Pals' trenches, contains 1,000 graves, of which 200 contain unidentified remains. A number of Bradford Pals are buried here, but carved on many headstones is just the running-horse insignia of the West Yorkshire Regiment. The three cemeteries on the Serre Road have a few Bradford Pals' graves, but not as many as one might expect, and some other nearby cemeteries do not seem to contain any graves of Bradford Pals at all. At first this is surprising, given the large numbers who were reportedly killed, until one realises that very many bodies from the battle were never recovered; the deadly effects of sustained artillery fire, in particular, would have meant that the identification of individual corpses was often well-nigh impossible.

As a memorial to the men whose bodies were never found, Sir Edwin Lutyens designed the impressive Thiepval Memorial to the Missing, which stands just a few miles to the north of Albert on rising ground, enabling it to be clearly visible for miles around. This monument, opened in 1932, has inscribed upon it the names of over 72,000 British and Commonwealth soldiers, 90 per cent of whom died between July and November 1916. The names of many of the Bradford Pals are on the monument.

A disaster on the home front

For many years the most notable monument in Scholemore Cemetery, Lidget Green, was in the form of a uniformed fireman, carved out of stone and standing on top of a massive stone plinth with a hosepipe in his hands. This memorial was unveiled in 1924, eight years after the incident that it commemorates. At the beginning of the twenty-first century the memorial was cleaned up and moved to stand outside the headquarters of the West Yorkshire Fire Service in Birkenshaw, on the other side of Bradford from Lidget Green and much closer to the scene of a particularly tragic wartime accident.

Shakespeare has Hamlet say that 'When sorrows come, they come not single spies, but in battalions.' The dreadful losses of the Somme had been preceded just a few weeks before by the Battle of Jutland, the only major sea battle of the First World War, in which the Royal Navy lost three battle cruisers, three cruisers and eight destroyers. Men from Bradford were killed in the battle; who actually won the engagement has never been determined. Hardly had the news of this sea battle been digested when news of the terrible Somme disaster arrived, soon to be followed by a catastrophe of a different kind and much nearer home. This would cause still more grief for the citizens of Bradford.

In 1916 what we would now call an industrial estate existed at Low Moor, about 4 miles from Bradford city centre, in the direction of Huddersfield. As we have seen in an earlier chapter, iron had been worked in this area for centuries, and at the beginning of the twentieth century the Low Moor Iron Company continued this tradition. Nearby was the Bradford Corporation Gas Works. Crucially, also on this site was the Low Moor Chemical Company, which by 1916 was under the auspices of the Ministry of Munitions. Before 1914 this factory had produced industrial dyes. During the war it switched to producing lyddite, an explosive compound derived from picric acid, which had formerly been used in Bradford's textile industry to dye silk. Lyddite was one of the main explosives used by the Royal Artillery in its shells, until it was superseded by TNT part-way through the war.

Memorial statue to firemen killed at Low Moor now outside West Yorkshire Fire Service HQ. (Sue Naylor)

With a gasworks and an ironworks in close proximity to a munitions factory producing explosives, the Low Moor site was, as we would say today, an accident waiting to happen. The serious consequences of any accident would certainly be increased because the Low Moor site was not at all in a remote location. Nearby were the neighbourhoods of Wyke, Odsal and Low Moor itself, all with their houses, schools, shops and churches.

The accident duly happened on the afternoon of 21 August 1916. According to the subsequent investigation and the coroner's report, a drum of picric acid burst into flames as it was being moved from one department of the chemical works to another. The fire quickly spread, the alarm was raised and most of the workers were able to be evacuated. But about fifteen minutes later there was a gigantic explosion, reminiscent perhaps of the mines that had been detonated under the German trenches at the start of the Somme offensive, just a few weeks earlier. This explosion was so loud that it was heard all over Bradford

and even in villages in Nidderdale, over 30 miles away. The chemical works had its own fire-fighting team, whose members were attempting to tackle the blaze when the explosion occurred. All were killed. Debris was scattered over a mile radius, some of it falling on one of the fire engines which were by now rushing towards Low Moor. Almost as soon as the first fire engine from Bradford arrived on the scene there was a second huge explosion. This killed six firemen and injured several others before they had even dismounted from their vehicle. A third explosion was caused when a gasholder of the Corporation Gas Works was ignited by flying debris. There were more explosions that afternoon and into the evening, over twenty in total. Fires burned on the site for most of the next two days.

Householders in nearby Low Moor and Wyke fled, some spending the next two nights in local woods. According to the report of the Bradford City surveyor, fifty houses were so badly damaged that they had to be demolished and 2,000 more needed repairs. A total of thirty-eight people lost their lives, far fewer than had at first been anticipated, given the magnitude and ferocity of the explosions.

Low Moor Iron Works, 1910. (Courtesy of Bradford Libraries)

Although the conclusion reached by the investigators was that the disaster was a tragic accident, some people leaped to the conclusion – eventually quashed – that the explosions and fires had been the work of spies and foreign agents. Certainly there were Belgian refugees in Bradford, some of whom worked at Low Moor, but the members of this group, who had fled their homeland when it was overrun by the Germans, would scarcely have committed such an act of sabotage against friendly allies who had offered them support and hospitality. And Bradford's German community, which otherwise might have come under suspicion, scarcely existed by 1916, as we shall now see.

Germans go home

When war broke out in August 1914 a common quip, apparently, was that many of the inhabitants of Bradford were unsure which side they were on. This is a reference to Bradford's German community, which, as has been described in an earlier chapter, had settled in the city in the nineteenth century and had contributed hugely to the city's commercial success as well as enhancing its civic and cultural life. Some members of this community had become naturalised British citizens by 1914 and several even served as officers in the British Army. The First Bradford Pals was itself commanded for a time by a man with German ancestry, Colonel G.H. Muller. However, others had retained their German nationality and some of the younger men were in fact German army reservists. A group of these left Bradford to join the Kaiser's forces as soon as war was declared, as the *Yorkshire Observer* reported on 5 August 1914: 'a number of young Germans residing in Bradford left the city in order to join their regiments ... They were seen off by friends and the German Pastor.' That they were also seen off at the station to the accompaniment of a German band may seem incredible nowadays, but the concept of total war was quite unfamiliar to people in 1914. Britain had not been involved in a European conflict since 1815. Consequently wars were seen as remote events, fought far away in the colonies or in distant foreign lands (and often by foreign allies and mercenaries rather than British troops). Before the industrial age a foreign war might scarcely impinge on people's everyday lives at all. Jane Austen's novels, for example, were written and are set during the Napoleonic period, yet the war is never mentioned. And it is said that at the

start of one eighteenth-century battle the English commander bowed to his French counterpart and politely invited him to fire first, almost as if warfare in those days was some kind of game in which it was only right to give your adversary a sporting chance. So it might have been that in the very first days of the First World War some old-fashioned ideas about fair play and chivalrous behaviour between enemies still prevailed – as also made evident by the famous Christmas truce of 1914. Thus the German band and the well-wishers on the station platform were tolerated.

If such an attitude existed on the home front at the time of the German reservists' departure, it certainly didn't last. At the end of August the Riot Act had to be read in Keighley, where for two nights German-owned shops were attacked and looted by

Memorial to Bradford Pals at Hébuterne near the Somme, France. (Sue Naylor)

a mob of mainly Irish immigrants who were only dispersed by police baton charges. German-owned shops in Bradford were also attacked, as anti-German feelings began to grow. The Kursaal baths in Morley Street were soon renamed the Windsor Baths, in order to shed the Germanic associations of the name. Windsor was, of course, a quintessentially English name and the British royal family, no less, adopted it in 1917, abandoning their German dynastic name of Saxe-Coburg-Gotha. The prestigious Bradford Club in Piece Hall Yard, to which many of Bradford's German textile merchants belonged, and which some had helped to found, now closed its doors to anyone of a German or Austrian background. Soon many German nationals had been arrested and they were interned (usually on the Isle of Man) for the duration of hostilities. Those who managed to avoid internment simply left Bradford and went back home to Germany. Their skills, business acumen and cultural sophistication went with them. So did their money.

War memorial, central Bradford. (Sue Naylor)

J.B. Priestley laments this loss in *English Journey* (1934):

I can remember when one of the best-known clubs in Bradford was the 'Schillerverein'. And in those days a Londoner was a stranger sight than a German ... Bradford was determinedly Yorkshire and provincial, yet some of its suburbs reached as far as Frankfurt and Leipzig. It was odd enough. But it worked. The war changed all that. There is hardly a trace now in the city of that German-Jewish invasion ... I liked the city better as it was before, and most of my fellow-Bradfordians agree with me. It seems smaller and duller now.

War industry

Bradford, like the other West Riding communities, contributed to the war effort, as one would expect, by turning out thousands upon thousands of uniforms for all branches of the services, as well as blankets and other items. At the end of 1914 the *Yorkshire Observer* could even boast: 'There has been no more wonderful and eventful year than that which is just drawing to a close in the whole history of the woollen industry.' This commercial activity was important, as it helped compensate for the loss of European markets. Bradford's well-established and lucrative textile trade with Germany, for example, naturally disappeared completely once war had been declared. The problem of what would happen once peace was restored and the army no longer needed its uniforms was still to be faced.

Other industries also contributed in smaller ways to the war effort. Despite the fact that Bradford is many miles from the nearest coastline, over sixty seaplanes were built by the Phoenix Dynamo Works at Thornbury during the war. Whether these primitive aeroplanes contributed very much to final victory is doubtful, though we know that some saw service in the Middle East and one may even have been responsible for the first ever sinking of a ship by an aircraft, when it torpedoed a small Turkish steamer near the Dardanelles.

Although Bradford's contribution to naval air power at this time may have been minor, at least the seaplane project appears to have had some success, which is more than can be said for the Scott Guncar. This was essentially a motorcycle with a machine-gun mounted on it. The vehicle was manufactured by a Bradford motorcycle firm and was an attempt to produce a weapon which combined mobility with fire-power. It proved to be far from effective. Although it was intended that several units would be equipped with the Guncar, it was withdrawn from service quite early in the war and never used on the battlefield.

Life on the home front in Bradford was not much dissimilar from what went on in other places throughout Britain. There were shortages, there were anxieties about family members serving in the armed forces and, because of rigid censorship, there was a chronic lack of accurate information in the press about how the war was progressing.

But the two aspects that turn this period into one of particular and major significance for Bradford were the deaths of so many of the city's young men on the Somme battlefield and the exodus of Bradford's unique German community. There were signs before 1914 that the worsted trade was entering a period of decline, mainly because of growing foreign competition and the effects of tariffs, but commerce and trade go through cycles of ebb and flow and in the past Bradford had always managed to weather the storms and retain its pre-eminent position. The Somme tragedy altered everything because it was responsible for the loss of so many able and energetic young men who would normally have helped Bradford to continue its remarkable progress. The departure of the German community was likewise of major importance, for it deprived the city of a group whose presence and influence had, since the mid-nineteenth century, been vital to the creation of a wealthy and vibrant city. After 1918 things would be more difficult.

Aftermath

Today, reminders of this dark wartime period exist mainly in the form of war memorials located throughout Bradford's suburbs and in nearby towns and villages. Bradford's principal war memorial, which stands in the centre of the city, was unveiled on 1 July 1922, fittingly the sixth anniversary of the first day of the Somme offensive. This obelisk is about 20ft high and made of local stone, with the usual *Pro Patria Mori* inscribed near the top (unintentionally hinting at what Wilfred Owen famously called 'the old lie' in his poem 'Dulce et Decorum Est'). At either side of the obelisk as you face it are two larger-than-life bronze figures, a soldier and a sailor, who look as if they are rushing forward, rifles in hand, to kill you. Originally this warlike pair had fixed bayonets, but apparently this was deemed to be too uncomfortable an image – too violent perhaps to commemorate all those who were slaughtered in a war – so the bayonets had

to be removed. From some angles the two men look as if they are about to over-balance and fall over, an unintended but maybe not entirely inappropriate memorial to the fallen.

Outside the National Media Museum on the other side of the road from the war memorial stands a superb modern statue of J.B. Priestley, pipe in hand and coat tails flapping. He has his back to the war memorial, which is perhaps only as it should be – as he was angered not just by his own experience of the war but also by the way former servicemen were treated afterwards. In *English Journey* he recounts how he attended a reunion dinner of the Duke of Wellington's regiment at the Market Tavern in Bradford in the early 1930s. He was understandably saddened that so many of his old comrades had been killed in the war and therefore would not be present, and he was strongly aware that some had only been able to attend because of the generosity of those who had paid for their meals. But what really shocked him was learning that some men had reluctantly declined the invitation because they did not have a decent suit – a terrible and shameful irony in a city that had helped to clothe the world; a city that proudly used to call itself Worstedopolis.

ten

PIONEERS AND REFORMERS

hat is particularly noteworthy about the people described in this chapter is that their achievements were very much shaped by the experience of living and working in Bradford. For example, it is doubtful whether Friederich Eurich would have defeated the scourge of anthrax if he had been living in, say, a mining community where the disease was unknown. Similarly, Margaret McMillan's pioneering work in education was directly related to her observation of the extreme deprivation in which many children in Bradford lived.

Defeating anthrax

Friederich Wilhelm Eurich (1867-1945) was born in Chemnitz, Saxony, and came to Bradford at the age of seven. As his name indicates, his family were members of Bradford's German community and his father worked for a German-owned firm of yarn spinners and exporters. Friederich attended Bradford Grammar School and then Edinburgh University, where he qualified as a doctor. He set up his medical practice back in Bradford in 1896 and also worked in Bradford hospitals, holding a free-of-charge surgery at Bradford Royal Infirmary on Saturday mornings.

Anthrax, the much-feared wool-sorters' disease, had been a major health problem in Bradford's textile industry since the 1840s. It was first noticed when alpaca and mohair started to be imported for use in worsted manufacturing. If spoors containing the anthrax bacteria were inhaled by workers handling infected fleeces, serious illness and a painful death often followed. Various precautionary measures were used, but these were often ineffective. By the end of the nineteenth century at least one case per week of anthrax was still being reported in Bradford and a third of these resulted in death.

White Abbey children's feeding centre, 1908. (Courtesy of Bradford Libraries)

In 1905 the Bradford Anthrax Investigation Board was established in Morley Street and Eurich was appointed as its bacteriologist. He began to devise new ways of eliminating infection from imported fleeces and skins and this led to the setting up of the Wool Disinfecting Station in Liverpool, where raw fleeces could be treated as soon as they entered the country and before they arrived in Bradford. The work he did for the Board over the next few years led to anthrax being largely eradicated in the textile industry and the Anthrax Prevention Act of 1918, which he helped to formulate, introduced stringent legal and medical measures to make sure that this deadly disease would never again be a threat to Bradford's textile workers (however, the Act did not deter various countries, including Britain, from developing lethal strains of anthrax for use as biological weapons. It was not until 1972 that such weapons were outlawed, after the Biological Weapons Convention was signed by all the major powers).

When Eurich died in 1945 the *Yorkshire Observer* published an obituary: '[He] did so much to conquer the disease of anthrax and [his] contributions in the cause of medicine were ... outstanding.'

Education for all

In his biography of Sir Charles Dilke, Roy Jenkins describes William Edward Forster (1818-86) as: 'A stubborn, irascible man with a great capacity for defying his constituents or anyone else who disagreed with him ... [he] shared with the Queen alone the great Victorian distinction of having a railway terminus named after him.' And one of Bradford's major squares too. Forster, MP for Bradford from 1861 until his death, held various important ministerial posts during his parliamentary career, including that of Chief Secretary for Ireland in Gladstone's second administration, but it is as the architect of the Elementary Education Act of 1870 that he is best remembered. This Act was – and still is – the foundation stone of the English maintained school system, and as such its importance cannot be overstated. Thomas Reid, Forster's biographer, understood the significance of the Act and the contribution of the man who had devised it: 'upon the day on which [Forster] stood up in the House of Commons to explain the scheme, born of his fertile brain and matured by his patient care and industry, for bringing to every child of English birth the blessing of education, he reached the highest point in his career as a patriot and a statesman'.

As early as 1850 Forster had outlined his ideas for a national system of education. At a public meeting in Bradford in that year he had received backing for a resolution which was sent to Parliament and which the *Bradford Observer* recorded in full:

> That this meeting, while it acknowledges with pleasure the vast efforts voluntarily made in the cause of education, and also the beneficial effects of the measures adopted by the Educational Committee of the Privy Council, is yet of the opinion that there is such a deficiency both of the quantity and the quality of the means of instruction as to demand more general and comprehensive arrangements; and would therefore urge upon Parliament the importance of meeting the wants of national education by devising such measures as are necessary for its extension and improvement on the principle of strict impartiality to all religious communions, and as far as possible on the basis of local management.

The meeting of 1850, according to the *Bradford Observer*, was unanimous in its enthusiasm for Forster's ideal of a national education system, but when his Act was passed twenty years later there was an apparent change of mood in the city. At a meeting in St George's Hall, at which the customary annual vote of thanks

was due to be given to the town's MPs, an amendment was passed disapproving of Forster's Act. In effect this was a vote of censure on Forster, whose response – measured and clear – showed an awareness of his fellow townspeople's traditional habit of offering blunt criticism and scant praise: 'You have only done what I have always expected Bradford people to do – to say what you think.' There were several reasons for the meeting's hostility to the Act. For some people it did not go far enough. The largest group of denominational schools, those under the auspices of the Church of England, were to remain completely intact and would continue to receive a subsidy from the Treasury. To the inhabitants of a town like Bradford, where most people were Nonconformists rather than Anglicans, this must have irked. Secularists also felt that too much had been conceded to the Established Church lobby. For others the Act went too far in another direction, for they could see that the creation of locally-administered school boards wherever there were gaps in provision could mean only one thing – an increase in the rates. And others were probably not convinced that the children of the labouring classes would require much of an education anyway, given that their likely future would consist of working as unskilled mill operatives and the like. But despite the initial hostility, Forster's Act was eventually to find favour in Bradford and throughout the rest of England.

For many years a bronze statue of Forster, unveiled in 1890, stood in the Bradford square that was named after him, close to the railway station that also bears his name. At the time of writing there are plans to place the statue once more in this part of the city centre, next to a proposed new shopping centre. Also in 1890 a second bronze statue of Forster was placed in the Victoria Embankment Gardens in London, outside what were then the offices of the London School Board. This one bears the following inscription: 'To his wisdom and courage England owes the establishment throughout the land of a national system of elementary education.'

The influence of Margaret McMillan

Jack Milner started work as a pupil-teacher in the first decade of the twentieth century and continued to teach in Bradford schools right up to his death in the 1960s. Towards the end of his life he vividly described the conditions at Usher Street and Feversham Street, the elementary schools where he had begun his career. These schools served some of the poorest neighbourhoods in Bradford

Municipal milk depot, 1923. (Courtesy of Bradford Libraries)

and most of the pupils only attended for half days; the other part of the day they worked a six-hour shift in the mills and as a consequence they often fell asleep at their desks. A few had boots to wear, most had clogs but there were always some who came to school barefoot, even in winter. Nearly all of the pupils, Jack remembered, had shiny patches on their cuffs; handkerchiefs were unknown. The smell of unwashed bodies, especially in wet weather, was always very strong. St James's wholesale fruit and vegetable market was near to both schools and pupils would often truant in order to steal whatever food they could from the stalls. The market employed a team of ex-policemen, equipped with canes, to move the truants on.

Teaching in these schools was exceedingly difficult, as most of the pupils (and their parents) resented compulsory attendance, for it meant a significant reduction in the family income if a child could only work in the mill part-time. This resentment could turn to violence; it was not unusual for teachers to be stoned as they left school and there were times when Jack and his colleagues had to use sticks to fight their way through jeering crowds of pupils who were waiting for them outside the school gate. Given these harsh working conditions, it is not surprising that the teachers in such schools were paid a sum of

£10 per annum as danger money in addition to their normal salaries. This was the harsh educational environment that Margaret McMillan sought to ameliorate during her stay in Bradford.

Margaret McMillan (1860-1931) was a Christian Socialist who was invited by the newly-formed Independent Labour Party to come, with her sister Rachel, and work in Bradford. As she wrote in *The Life of Rachel McMillan* (1927): 'on a stormy night in November 1893. Coming out from the entrance of the Midland Station we saw, in a swither of rain, the shining statue of Oastler standing in Market Square, with two black and bowed little mill workers standing at his knee. Through an opening, as we climbed the hill beyond the Station Hotel, the wind rushed out like a wolf.'

Margaret McMillan lived in Bradford until 1902, at which time her health began to suffer because of over-work, and she departed to live in the south of England, where she recovered her health and continued her pioneering work, notably in Deptford. Despite her comparatively short stay in the city, she was able, as a member of the Bradford School Board, to initiate a series of far-sighted, pioneering measures aimed at improving the lives of Bradford's

Green Lane School kitchen, 1908. (Courtesy of Bradford Libraries)

schoolchildren. Concerned that many children were physically weak and unfit, she worked with the headteacher of Wapping School, William Sykes, to establish a swimming bath at the school, and this opened in 1898. It was probably the first swimming pool in any maintained school in the country. A second school pool was opened at Green Lane School in 1903, and others were built a little later at Drummond Road and Grange Road schools.

The School Board had appointed a school medical officer as early as 1893, and Margaret McMillan worked with him to establish regular medical inspections for all Bradford schoolchildren, the first of which took place at Usher Street School in 1899, with Margaret McMillan in attendance. Again, this initiative was probably the first of its kind in the country. One consequence of the Usher Street inspection was the discovery that more than 100 of the children inspected had not removed their clothes for between six and eight months. Jack Milner remembered that under their clothes throughout the winter months some children would be wrapped in a layer of brown paper covered in Stockholm tar and this would not be removed until the warmer spring weather arrived.

Horrified by such practices, Margaret McMillan set about educating parents about hygiene and health and she also urged the Corporation to provide more public baths in the city. She was also keen to ensure that children were better fed. Sykes, the headteacher of Wapping School, had already begun to provide school meals for his poorest pupils as early as 1886, relying on donations from well-wishers and local philanthropists. Encouraged by this, Margaret McMillan campaigned for school meals to be available throughout the city. Eventually this led to the establishment of a municipal school meals service in 1907. A central kitchen was built at Green Lane School, from which meals were distributed to other schools. The head of Green Lane at the time was Jonathan Priestley, whose son J.B. Priestley believed that his father was operating the first such initiative in Britain, as he wrote in the preface to his biography of Fred Jowett (1946): 'It was at my father's school that the first children in the country received school meals and we knew all about it at home because this piece of social service, considered a revolutionary step then, attracted a good deal of attention in both the local and national press.'

Margaret McMillan agitated for a range of other educational reforms, such as better facilities for handicapped children and the provision of free nursery education. However, because of the First World War it was not until the early 1920s that Bradford Council opened its first three nursery schools, at St Anne's Broomfields, Princeville and Lilycroft. At Lilycroft the charismatic superinten-

Lilycroft Board School, 1874. (Courtesy of Bradford Libraries)

dent Miriam Lord developed nursery education so successfully that, according to the school logbook, teachers and educational officials from many countries came to learn from her, and she was invited to deliver lectures on her work to educationists at several overseas universities. Like Margaret McMillan, Miriam Lord has had her pioneering work commemorated by having one of Bradford's primary schools named after her. Margaret McMillan College, for the training of teachers, was also established in Bradford. Later this became the McMillan School of Teaching, Health and Care, a part of Bradford College and named in honour of Bradford's – and possibly the country's – most influential advocate of a better education for the children of the poor. As Margaret McMillan wrote:

The condition of the poorer children is worse than anything which was described or painted. It was a thing which this generation is glad to forget. The neglect of infants, the utter neglect almost of toddlers and older children, the blight of early labour, all combined to make of a once vigorous people a race of undergrown and spoiled adolescents; and just as people looked on at the torture two hundred years ago and less, without any great indignation, so in the 1890s people saw the misery of poor children without perturbation.

She made people more aware of the need to tackle the problems she describes here, and as the twentieth century started to unfold Bradford became nationally known for its promotion of educational reforms. In 1916 the Bradford Trades Council produced the Bradford Charter, which proposed that the school leaving age should be raised to sixteen and that secondary education in the city should be free and available to all. Some parts of the Charter were adopted by the government of the day and became part of the 1918 Education Act, which abolished the half-time system, permitted the abolition of secondary-school fees and raised the school leaving age to fourteen (it was not until the 1970s that the leaving age was raised to sixteen).

Margaret McMillan. (Courtesy of Bradford Libraries)

One of Margaret McMillan's colleagues on the School Board was James Hanson (1815-95) a prominent member of the Liberal Party in Bradford. In the early 1890s he persuaded the Board to set up several higher-grade schools, which were the precursors of Bradford's municipal secondary grammar schools. These were the first of their kind in the country. One of them – now a secondary comprehensive school – was named after Hanson.

Gadie's Folly

Not all of Bradford's reformers and pioneers were socialists like Margaret McMillan or Liberals like W.E. Forster and James Hanson. Anthony Gadie (1868-1948), who served on Bradford Council from 1900 to 1945 and was MP for Bradford Central between 1924 and 1929, was a life-long Conservative. Gadie was initially a builder and he first made his name in 1910 by developing what was known as Gadie's Garden Suburb in Allerton. By the twentieth century places like Allerton, on the outskirts of Bradford, had become more accessible by public transport, and better-off families were moving away from the heavily-polluted central areas of Bradford to healthier and more salubrious suburban neighbourhoods.

But Gadie's crowning glory was still to come. He became the chairman of the city's Water Committee in 1921 and set about addressing a problem from which Bradford had suffered for a century – a shortage of water. Some progress had been made in the nineteenth century to ensure a better supply (see Chapter Six) and Angram reservoir was built between 1904 and 1919 in upper Nidderdale to supply the city. Despite this, the problem persisted. Gadie's plan was to build a second, larger, reservoir a short distance below Angram. Work on Scar House reservoir commenced in 1921 and was completed in 1936 at a cost of over £8 million. The reservoir dam, 233ft high, was for some years the highest masonry dam in Europe.

Just as Forster had met with opposition in Bradford when he pioneered elementary education for all, likewise Gadie came in for criticism during the construction of Scar House. Some believed the project was far too expensive and dismissed it as 'Gadie's Folly'. However, severe droughts in 1933 and 1934 made people realise that Scar House was very necessary if Bradford was to

Manchester Road baths, 1905. (Courtesy of Bradford Libraries)

Scar House reservoir, Nidderdale. (Sue Naylor)

overcome the problem of water shortage. Gadie was knighted in 1935 and received the freedom of the city in 1946. When he died two years later the *Yorkshire Observer* said this of him: 'Sir Anthony rose from very humble circumstances to be the most influential public man in Bradford.'

Fred Jowett and municipal housing

It is generally agreed that the Boundary Estate in Bethnal Green, opened by London County Council in 1900, was the country's first municipal housing project. Bradford Council soon followed this lead, mainly because of the efforts of Fred Jowett (1864-1944), the first socialist to have a seat on Bradford Council following his election in 1892. Jowett was one of the founders of the Independent Labour Party (see Chapter Eight) and later became an MP. Improving housing conditions for the poor was just one of his concerns – he also worked with Margaret McMillan to promote better education and welfare for children – and in 1909 Bradford's first municipal housing scheme was completed. Just as the Boundary Estate was built in one of the worst slum areas in London, so the Longlands Improvement Area was situated in Goitside, the intention being that families from the Goitside and White Abbey slums would be the beneficiaries. The Council cleared some slum properties and erected five blocks of three-storey tenements on Longlands Street and followed these with more on Chain Street and Roundhill Place. It was a modest beginning and there were still many members of the Council who were unsure about the wisdom of the initiative, believing that private philanthropy might be a better option. Others, sensibly, understood that a philanthropist like Titus Salt, prepared to finance sound family housing out of his own personal fortune, only comes along very occasionally.

After the First World War the government saw that people like Jowett were right and that municipalities should be pro-active in providing rented accommodation. The Housing Act of 1919 gave councils financial incentives to build houses and Bradford Corporation responded by building more than 10,000 council houses between then and the outbreak of the Second World War. That figure represented almost 50 per cent of the houses built in the city in that period. Jowett's campaigning had been vindicated.

eleven

THE START OF A LONG DECLINE?

The export trade of such places as Bradford was declining long before the [First World] War ... You cannot expect to teach other people to make goods and then expect them to go on still buying those goods from you.

J.B. Priestley, English Journey (1934)

At the time those words were written few people would have disagreed with the author. The commercial activity that had thrust Bradford into the limelight – the worsted cloth trade – had been in decline since the 1880s, but most people did not recognise this until after 1918. The phenomenal commercial success that Bradford had enjoyed throughout the middle decades of the nineteenth century and the civic self-confidence this had engendered led in many quarters to a belief that trade and industry remained healthy and strong and probably always would. This illusion about the state of the city's commerce continued as if under its own impetus until the First World War, rather as a steam train carries on rolling along the tracks for quite a time after the steam has been cut off.

The war changed everything, not just in Bradford but in Britain as a whole (and indeed Europe). An entire generation of young men had been killed in the war and the cost of the conflict brought the country close to bankruptcy. In addition, in Bradford's case, as described in Chapter Nine, many of the German merchants who had been so influential in making the city prosperous had left. As Priestley wrote: 'That fairy tale of trade has been rudely concluded ... Everybody in the business I talked to confirmed this ...'

Crowther Court slum area, 1930s. (Courtesy of Bradford Libraries)

The economy

Immediately after the war, though, things looked rather good. There was even a mini-boom in Britain's economy, but it did not last. In Bradford things soon went into serious decline. In 1920 Britain's worsted exports were worth about £140 million; the following year they were worth only £62 million; and although they recovered to £90 million in 1924 they had declined again by the late 1920s. The Wall Street Crash of 1929 had a catastrophic effect on the world economy, and in 1930 and 1931 British worsted exports were scarcely worth £30 million a year. A partial recovery by the late 1930s meant that this figure had risen to £45 million, but this was a far cry from the 1920 position and light years away from the heady days before 1914.

Because exports were so vital to Bradford's economy, the government's decision (instigated by Winston Churchill in 1925) to return to the Gold Standard had very serious implications, for it led to the pound being overvalued. Overseas customers had to pay for British goods in sterling, so an overvalued pound meant that exports now became more expensive. Naturally this led foreign customers to buy fewer goods from their British suppliers or seek cheaper alternatives produced in other countries. Faced with this reduction in exports, the manufacturers in Bradford followed the example set by Lister thirty years earlier; they responded to the crisis by proposing a cut in wages of 10 per cent. The employees, who understandably wished to retain their wartime wage rates, went on strike. The 1925 strike involved 150,000 workers at all levels of the industry (other than management) throughout West Yorkshire. It had a good deal of public support. At one stage the Lord Mayor of Bradford and the Archbishop of York intervened in an attempt to negotiate a settlement, but to no avail. Eventually a public enquiry recommended that the cuts should not take place and reluctantly the employers agreed. But it was only a temporary victory for the workers. Given the unfavourable economic conditions, sooner or later something would have to give.

For the time being, however, it seemed that the umbrella organisation for the textile workers, the National Association of Unions in the Textile Trade, first formed in 1917, had achieved a notable success. And although the Association was not called upon to bring its members out during the General Strike the following year, the textile workers did offer firm support, both moral and financial, to those who actually took industrial action. Bradford's railway workers, printers and tram workers went on strike, but there was little unrest or violence in the city during the dispute, although a handful of Communist Party members were arrested in Shipley. Neither was there much blacklegging. The popular image of upper-class chaps (like the character in Evelyn Waugh's *Brideshead Revisited*) enjoying themselves as strike-breakers by driving about in trams and buses did not apply in Bradford.

The General Strike only lasted nine days, although the miners, in support of whom the strike had originally been called, continued to strike for several months. Few people came out of the dispute with much credit, least of all the leadership of the Labour Party, which failed to give support to the strikers for fear of appearing to be seen as endorsing a possible revolution. On the other hand, the king expressed some sympathy for the strikers.

Unemployment

Unemployment in Bradford rose throughout the 1920s, peaking in the early 1930s. In 1923, 8 per cent of Bradford's workforce was unemployed, and by 1925 this had risen to over 9 per cent. In 1931, at the worst point of the Great Depression, a shocking 35,000 men and women were unemployed in Bradford. As things improved throughout the 1930s this figure fell to 21,500 in 1938 and to about 10,500 the following year. But in 1930 things were bad, and the employers once more proposed a reduction in wages. This again led to a strike. It was a failure and although employees in some firms did not suffer a cut, in

Market Street 1949. (Courtesy of Bradford Libraries)

others workers had to stomach a reduction of as much as 20 per cent over a two-year period. There was great hardship and the irony was, of course, that many people, unemployed or on short-time, walked Bradford's streets in shabby and threadbare clothes not because the warehouses were empty but because they were crammed full of high-quality worsted cloth for which there was no market.

Bad as unemployment was in Bradford, especially in the early 1930s, it never reached the level experienced by communities in the North-East of England, or in some of the cotton towns of Lancashire. There was never an equivalent of a Jarrow Crusade or the publication of a book like Walter Greenwood's *Love on the Dole* (1933), which brought the plight of the unemployed in other parts of the North to a wider audience. Anticipating Norman Tebbit's oft-quoted piece of advice uttered in the 1980s, some unemployed people left Bradford to seek work in the Midlands and the South (though not necessarily on their bikes, as Tebbit's father supposedly had done). The exodus was not as significant as that from some Lancashire communities, but it was a telling contrast with the situation just a few decades earlier, when people had flocked to Bradford in their thousands looking for work in a town where industry was booming.

There were unemployment benefits in the 1930s, but these were hardly adequate and the financial crisis of 1931 meant that they were reduced by 10 per cent and could only be claimed for twenty-six weeks. After that, claimants had

Back-to-back houses in 1930s (Laisteridge Court). (Courtesy of Bradford Libraries)

to undergo a means test; any savings or valuables or wages from other family members were assessed before an unemployed person could receive anything at all. The means test was universally loathed.

Even those who had a job in Bradford's textile industry were not well paid, especially in comparison with what it had been possible to earn in the boom years of the mid-nineteenth century, when wages in textiles tended to be higher than the national average. By the 1930s they were about 5 per cent lower. Nationally a wage of £5 a week was considered good and £4 adequate; in Bradford £4 was considered good and £3 just about acceptable. These pay rates applied to men; traditionally women had made up a large percentage of Bradford's workforce and their average wages were much lower: £1 10s was common, rising to £2 if a woman was involved in piece-work. It has been estimated that about 40 per cent of women in Bradford were employed or seeking work in the 1930s. As we shall see, after 1945 many women were reluctant to return to low-paid work in the mills because they had enjoyed much better pay in munitions factories during the Second World War.

Reasons for the decline

Between 1928 and 1932 approximately 400 of Bradford's textile firms went out of business. Obviously the worldwide slump in trade was a major reason for this, but there were other important factors too. As J.B. Priestley noted, it was unreasonable to assume that foreign competitors would never be able to capture Bradford's overseas markets. Japan, for example, had been in the process of extremely rapid industrialisation since the late nineteenth century and had become a serious competitor in textiles by 1930. Some colonies in the British Empire were also beginning to compete. Hattersley's, the Keighley firm of textile engineers, opened a plant in India to build machines for the burgeoning Indian textile industry. Such a move might have been good business for Hattersley's, but it is unlikely to have benefited any of Bradford's textile exporters.

These challenges from overseas showed one thing very clearly; much of Bradford's textile industry was actually inefficient. For a start there were too many small firms. Two-thirds of textile workers in the West Riding were working in firms that had fewer than 500 employees. Many of the firms were family-run and outsiders – no matter how competent – were not necessarily made welcome. Old-fashioned attitudes to management were common and there was often a reluctance to innovate or take risks. The great textile barons of the Victorian era – men like Salt and Lister – had succeeded because they were always aware of the need to adopt new techniques, design new machinery or use new materials. The creation of Saltaire was a huge – albeit calculated – gamble, as was Lister's endeavour to produce a yarn from silk waste. These men were never complacent or timid. The same could not always be said of their twentieth-century successors, who often appeared content to operate from outmoded buildings, using outmoded machinery and methods. Research was neglected and there was a suspicion, almost amounting to hostility, about the new artificial fibres, such as rayon, that had become available. Titus Salt, one imagines, would have been the first in the field to exploit the new fibres.

Despite the decline Bradford, with its Wool Exchange, remained the international centre of the worsted trade and 38 per cent of the city's working population was still employed in textiles in 1937. Firms engaged in wool-combing and top-making (producing combed long fibres for spinning into yarn) were able to continue competing in the export market with some success. Other firms found it much more difficult, and they turned increasingly to the domestic market. They were helped by a series of protectionist measures that the government enacted in the early 1930s and which by the mid-1930s had done much to eliminate foreign textile imports. Who knows how this would have gone down with the early Victorian textile magnates, for whom the concept of free trade had almost the status of a religious dogma! Then again, those men were nothing if not pragmatic and so they would probably have adjusted their beliefs and practices accordingly.

The 1930s: increasing prosperity for some

Bradford textile firms that had survived the difficult period of the late 1920s and early 1930s now began to exploit a domestic market which was actually growing. While the enduring image of the 1930s may be that of a period of unrelenting gloom, best illustrated by George Orwell's series of essays in *The Road to Wigan Pier*, the reality for many people was rather different. The Depression and its aftermath had little impact on communities and individuals not reliant on traditional industries. Overall, the standard of living rose in Britain as the 1930s went on. People had more money to spend on what became known as consumer goods, including clothing purchased from chainstores such as Marks and Spencer. Selling cloth directly to British retailers or to multiple tailors, such as Burton's, did not fully compensate Bradford's manufacturers for the loss of overseas markets, but it helped.

Even in Bradford there were some signs of growing affluence, provided that one was not unemployed or a textile worker on short-time. It has been estimated that there were fewer than 14,000 white-collar workers in Bradford in 1921; by the early 1930s the number had risen to about 25,000, and these people were generally better paid than mill-workers. The members of this growing clerical and administrative class were employed by such concerns as building societies and mail-order companies, two of which, Grattan Warehouse and Empire Stores, were set up in Bradford by members of the Fattorini family. Engineering firms, such as Hepworth and Grandage, English Electric and Crofts were less affected by the slump than were Bradford's textile firms. They continued to operate successfully throughout the inter-war period and provide employment. Bradford even had its own motor-car manufacturer, Jowett, located in the suburb of Idle. It had a workforce of about 1,000, which was producing 100 vehicles a week by the late 1930s. The fact that by this time car ownership was becoming a reality for many families indicates again that many people in Britain were becoming more prosperous. And gone was the time, pre-1914, when an eminent industrialist could solemnly offer the ludicrous opinion that mass-ownership of the motor-car was very unlikely because it would be impossible to train the required number of chauffeurs!

More people were taking holidays too. For those Bradford families who could afford it this usually meant a week at Scarborough on the Yorkshire coast or at the Lancashire resort of Morecambe. A shorter working week also meant more opportunities for watching sport. Cricket was particularly popular and the Bradford League, founded in 1903, had a national reputation for producing international players of repute, such as Herbert Sutcliffe and Len Hutton. County cricket was played at Park Avenue. There were two Football League clubs in the city as well as professional Rugby League clubs in Bradford and Keighley.

Bradford had a strong theatrical tradition rooted in nineteenth-century music halls and professional and amateur productions continued to be popular in Bradford in the inter-war period. The city's principal theatre, the Alhambra, had been opened in 1914, but the most famous event in the city's theatre history had occurred a few years earlier. On 13 October 1905 England's most famous actor, Sir Henry Irving, appeared in a production of *Beckett* at the Theatre Royal in Manningham Lane. The final curtain fell immediately after Irving (as Beckett) uttered the character's dying words, 'Into thy hands ...'. Later that evening Irving himself died at the Midland Hotel, where he was staying with his personal assistant, Bram Stoker, the celebrated author of *Dracula*. A small plaque on the wall of the hotel commemorates this event, and a battered suitcase, purporting to be Stoker's, is exhibited in one of the hotel corridors.

Dance halls were popular between the wars, especially with the young, but it was the cinema that really flourished at this time. By 1939 there were more than forty picture-houses in Bradford, and 'going to the pictures' had become the main leisure pursuit for many families.

Housing, health and politics

There were other signs that, for some people at least, Bradford was becoming a healthier and more amenable place. The 1924 Housing Act enabled some of the worst inner-city slums, such as those in White Abbey, to be cleared and replaced with council housing. New estates were built in Whetley Lane, Canterbury Avenue and at Ravenscliffe, with Scholemoor in Lidget Green

Derelict mill building in Little Horton Lane, mid-twentieth century. (Courtesy of British Libraries)

following shortly afterwards. For the more affluent, Heaton had replaced Manningham as the most desirable part of Bradford in which to live, though the really wealthy had by this time moved out of Bradford altogether and settled in places such as Ilkley or Harrogate, from where they were able to commute by rail or motor-car. There were even some who went to live as far away as Morecambe. A well-appointed train, with provision for a sumptuous breakfast, conveyed wealthy men every day to their businesses in Bradford.

The Corporation, in spite of being short of money, continued to make progress in the field of health. The former workhouse in Little Horton Lane had become a Poor Law hospital and then, after 1920, became the first municipal general hospital outside London. By 1939 a quarter of all births in Bradford took place there. A team of municipal midwives – possibly the first in the country – had already been formed as early as 1917 to assist women who chose to give birth at home. In 1936 the Royal Infirmary was moved from its original location at the junction of Lumb Lane and Westgate to a new suburban site in Duckworth Lane. Byelaws were enacted giving the Corporation more powers

to inspect bakeries, butchers and milk suppliers. This meant an end to such traditional practices as adulterating sugar with silver sand or boiling oranges to make them appear larger. But probably the most important public health advance concerned domestic sewage disposal. By 1939 almost all the earth closets in the city's houses had been replaced with water closets, thus ending the threat of deadly diseases caused by the unsanitary conditions that had been a feature of Bradford life in the previous century, especially in the slum areas.

After 1927 a significant part of the city centre was re-fashioned, with office blocks such as Britannia House eventually replacing warehouses. New shops, like the Art Deco styled Co-operative Society Emporium and new shopping streets, such as Broadway, appeared. By 1940 there were over 40 miles of trolley-bus routes to complement the 20 or so miles of tramway (trolley-buses were more effective than trams on the hillier routes). In addition there were over 70 miles of motor-bus routes. The central areas of Bradford were certainly still heavily polluted with smoke, but improvements in public transport and an increase in leisure time meant that it was easier for people to get into the nearby countryside and visit places such as Shipley Glen and Ilkley Moor.

With regard to politics, Bradford leaped into national prominence in 1936 at the time of the abdication crisis. Dr Blunt, the Bishop of Bradford, made a speech in which he referred to the king's 'need for grace'. Although Blunt was later to deny that the remark was in any way a reference to the monarch's affair with Mrs Simpson, his words were seized upon by the national press and within a fortnight Edward had abdicated. Apart from this highlight, the political scene in Bradford between the wars was characterised by a high degree of apathy, so much so that between 1931 and 1936 a fifth of the candidates at local elections were returned unopposed. The Liberals were no longer the great power they had been in nineteenth-century Bradford, and both Labour and the Conservatives benefited from the Liberal Party's decline. Although there were times when the Labour Party had the largest number of seats on Bradford Council, the Conservatives and Liberals usually formed an anti-socialist alliance to prevent them from taking power. However, the Labour Party in Bradford steadily increased its percentage of the vote at national elections. Labour was helped by the adoption of a more pragmatic approach, which superseded the utopian idealism of the Independent Labour Party. The link with the ILP was finally severed in 1932, and Labour's new and more cautious policies were succinctly summed up in 1935 by a writer in the *Bradford Pioneer*: 'we are neither extravagant nor perverse ... our programme brings direct ame-

Rush hour in Norfolk Street, 1954. (Courtesy of Bradford Libraries)

lioration to simple people ... blazing hearths, busy playing fields and peace of mind.' Hardly the stuff of revolution. And neither the Communist Party nor the British Union of Fascists had any impact in Bradford at this time. Extremism was not what people wanted.

The Second World War

'I returned the other afternoon to my native city of Bradford ... it was astonishing to discover that the familiar large drapers store and the old chapel were no longer there, and that in their place were some blackened ruins ...' So said J.B. Priestley in a BBC radio broadcast in August 1940. In fact Bradford got off lightly. Whereas other British cities and towns were severely damaged by the Luftwaffe's bombing campaign of 1940-41, Bradford only suffered a few raids, most of which were comparatively minor. At the time a strange rumour circulated that the city was being spared the full force of the blitz because of its traditional links with Germany. People pointed to the number of Bradford firms that still bore German names and nodded sagely. A post-war rumour even postulated that Bradford was left largely intact because the man who would have become *Gauleiter* of Britain, had the Nazis won the war, was born in Bradford. Wilhelm Bohle was indeed born in 1903 of German stock at an address in Bertram Road in Manningham. However, he was only three years old when his family left Bradford, so it is very unlikely that a sentimental attachment to his birthplace caused him to exert any influence on Goering's bombing strategy.

Air raids

There were three air raids on Bradford in August 1940. The first of these took place on the night of 22 August; three bombs were dropped harmlessly into Heaton Woods. Six days later there was another raid, this time rather better aimed at the city centre. There were no casualties and little damage was done, though St Peter's church in Leeds Road was hit and so were several shops.

A much heavier raid was launched on 31 August. This time German aircraft were over Bradford from about a quarter-past eleven until almost three o'clock the next morning. Lingards drapery store (the shop mentioned by Priestley) was destroyed, as was part of Rawson Market and a mill in Nelson Street. The Odeon cinema, then at the bottom of Manchester Road, was hit – fortunately the audience had left. An incendiary bomb landed in Wapping School swimming pool and was thus immediately extinguished, although a nearby factory that produced sulphuric acid was less fortunate, and was partially destroyed.

Maps captured from the Germans after the war seem to indicate that a target for the raid may have been the Phoenix engineering works at

Rawson Market bomb damage, 1940.
(Courtesy of Bradford Libraries)

Thornbury. Certainly a bomb landed on the West Bowling golf course, which was not too far away. The bomb crater was soon incorporated into the course as a new bunker, aptly named Hitler's Bunker, though nobody at the time could have foreseen the dramatic associations the name would have in the final weeks of the war. About 120 bombs in total were dropped in the raid, a mixture of incendiaries and high explosives. It is likely that the aircraft were Heinkel 111s, based in Norway, from where they would have crossed the North Sea to make a landfall near Hull. They would then have navigated by following the tributaries of the River Humber into the industrial areas of Yorkshire and beyond. The raid caused significant damage to the city, but only one, possibly two people were killed, although over 100 were injured.

There were no further raids until 14 March 1941, when bombs damaged houses across the city and some railway buildings in Clayton. On 5 May in the same year a German aircraft crashed into the High Street in Idle, killing three people and injuring five. There were no further raids of any significance on Bradford after that.

Women at war

There was, as noted earlier, a long tradition of women working in Bradford's textile industry. Consequently, when war broke out an experienced female workforce, used to long hours of tedious factory work, was ready to assist the war effort. A distinct advantage which Britain had over the enemy was a policy of directing all able-bodied women (other than those with children under fifteen years of age) into war-work or the uniformed services. Nazi ideology, on the other hand, insisted that women were to have no role other than that of housewife and child-bearer. The women of Germany were therefore never mobilised like the women of Britain.

For example, the AVRO plant at Yeadon, next to what is now Leeds and Bradford Airport, employed 17,500 people during the war, of whom 60 per cent were women, working twelve-hour shifts. The usual shift pattern consisted of two weeks on days followed by two weeks on nights. During the course of the war the plant produced 4,000 Avro Anson aircraft and 695 Lancaster bombers. Two-thirds of the workers at the Royal Ordnance factory at Steeton were women. This factory produced a total of 63 million shells during the war and received a visit from the king and queen in March 1942. Stell's engineering

Wellington Street, 1950s, showing poverty and dereliction. (Courtesy of Bradford Libraries)

plant in Keighley had 3,500 wartime employees, of whom 1,300 were women. Some firms completely changed their products. Lister and Co., for example, stopped producing velvet at the giant Manningham Mills and started to make Resilitex, a rubber substitute made from animal fibres and used for camouflage. Silk fabric for parachutes was also produced at Manningham Mills. Sharps Printers (later to become Hallmark Greeting Cards) in Bingley Road was taken over by a Coventry-based engineering firm engaged in war-work. Firms like these relied heavily on Bradford women throughout the war.

Communities contributed to the war effort in numerous ways. During War Weapons Week in May 1941 the townspeople of prosperous Ilkley raised £800,000 – a national record. As part of another campaign the iron railings surrounding Bradford's parks were removed and households were asked to relinquish metal pans so that weapons could be made. After the war it was revealed that most of the household metal collected was of little or no practical use for the war effort, although the campaign may have helped to boost morale by giving an impression that everybody was doing their bit to help achieve victory.

Refugees and prisoners

Before the war 400 Basque children, refugees from the Spanish Civil War, had been housed in a camp near East Morton. More refugees arrived in the Bradford area during the Second World War, notably a large group of children and young women from Guernsey, which was occupied by the Germans in 1940. Bradford families were given 5s per week if they agreed to give food and shelter to these refugees. Other families offered regular hospitality to Allied service personnel, such as Polish airmen, who for obvious reasons no longer had homes to go to when they were on leave. After the war some of these men settled in Bradford.

A prisoner-of-war camp was opened just outside Otley towards the end of the war, at a time when many thousands of German servicemen were surrendering to the British and American forces in Europe. The inmates were not repatriated until 1948, when the camp finally closed. Some of them were employed in building an estate of prefabricated houses (colloquially known as

Back-to-backs Jonas Gate, 1930s. (Courtesy of British Libraries)

prefabs) in Clayton. These temporary dwellings were eventually replaced with permanent houses in the 1950s. One of the Germans, Gunter R., settled in Bradford on his release from Otley and married a young Bradford woman. In 2011, still a Bradford resident, he recalled his time working on the Clayton prefabs and especially some conversations he had with Britain's most famous hangman, Albert Pierrepoint, who at the time was living in Clayton, close to the building site. On one occasion Pierrepoint informed Gunter that he was about to go to Germany to carry out some particularly important work. This work was, of course, the execution of the Nazi war criminals who had been found guilty at the Nuremberg war trials.

In common with people throughout Britain, the citizens of Bradford were greatly relieved when the war drew to an end. When VE Day was celebrated on 9 May 1945, the *Telegraph and Argus* carried the following report: 'Something of a carnival spirit pervaded the atmosphere. Folk let themselves go and even policemen on duty joined in the dancing.' The hard-won victory against Nazi Germany certainly merited dancing in the streets. Whether there would much to dance about in Bradford in the post-war era was less certain.

twelve

TOWARDS A MULTI-ETHNIC CITY

I n common with the rest of Britain, Bradford entered a period of austerity when the Second World War ended in 1945. The country was victorious but exhausted. There was an acute housing shortage and money for investment was hard to obtain. Many things were still rationed and remained so until the 1950s. The severe winter of 1947 disrupted the country's transport system, while a coal shortage led to frequent power cuts. But it was also a time of far-reaching social reforms. The railways and the coal mines were nationalised, the National Health Service was established and welfare provisions were improved. As a consequence of the 1944 Education Act secondary schools were reformed and local authority grants were made available for those wishing to study at university. For the first time it was possible for a person to progress right through the English education system and obtain a university degree without having to pay a penny.

Trade and industry

In the immediate post-war years Bradford's textile trade had a brief advantage over some of its traditional competitors. Industry in Japan and Germany was in ruins and large areas of northern France and Belgium, where textile industries were located, had also been severely disrupted, particularly in the later stages of the war. It could have been a golden opportunity for Bradford, and indeed in 1948 British wool and worsted exports, at £58 million, were better than they had been in the late 1930s. But this success was only temporary and in the years that followed Bradford's trade could not maintain its short-lived pre-eminent position either in the export market or closer to home. There was to be no return to the halcyon days of the nineteenth century and there were reasons for this. For a start the domestic market, which had become more important in the

immediate pre-war period, was now comparatively depressed. Most British people did not
have a great deal of money to spend on clothing and fabrics until the more affluent era of
the late 1950s and 1960s, by which time the
days when Bradford's trade had an advantage
had passed.

There were other reasons too. American
aid soon helped to revitalise the industries
of our erstwhile enemies and equip them
with modern factories and machinery.
Germany, shattered in 1945, underwent a
Wirtschaftswunder (economic miracle), such
that the Federal Republic was Europe's leading economy by the 1960s. France, defeated

Polish war memorial. (Sue Naylor)

and occupied in the war, had its *Trentes
Glorieuses*, a thirty-year period (1945-75) during which it too developed a
highly successful economy. Japan, once a sworn foe, was now regarded by the
USA as an important ally in the ideological struggle against Communist China
and the USSR and so was heavily financed by American capital. As a consequence all aspects of Japanese industry expanded at an astonishing rate in the
1950s and 1960s. Meanwhile British trade and industry, including Bradford's,
lagged behind.

In textiles there was also fierce competition from places like India, where
labour costs were low, and after the war the price of raw wool increased, which
added to costs in the UK. Many Bradford firms were also forced to use out-
dated machinery; because of the need to maintain foreign currency reserves it
was often impossible for British textile manufacturers to purchase more efficient machines from abroad and so maintain the necessary competitive edge.
Economy of scale was also a problem; there were still too many small textile
firms in the Bradford area. For example, even as late as 1972 three-quarters of
local firms engaged in processing textile waste had fewer than forty employees.

As the 1950s and 1960s progressed Bradford's textile industry was therefore once more in decline. There were over 1,200 textile firms in the city in
1950; by 1967 there were scarcely 800, and between 1951 and 1971 the workforce engaged in textiles had been reduced by 50 per cent. By the mid-1970s
half of Bradford's textile firms had been incorporated into fifteen companies,

such as Illingworth, Morris, which was the last textile firm to operate from Salts Mill.

In order once more for Bradford to prosper its trade and industry needed to be less reliant on textiles. As we have seen in earlier chapters, at the outset of the Industrial Revolution and well into the nineteenth century, coal mining, stone quarrying and iron working were all important local industries. There was even a suggestion at one time that Bradford should have a Stone Exchange because of the importance of the trade. In the twentieth century several engineering concerns, such as Hepworth and Grandage and English Electric, were established in Bradford and these offered an alternative to the textile industry. In the early 1950s International Harvester opened a factory at Idle, using the site of the defunct Jowett motor company (which went out of business in 1954). Bradford was also home to several printing concerns, chemical works, mail-order firms and building societies.

However, the overriding problem throughout the twentieth century was that there was never enough of this kind of diversification. People associated Bradford with woollen textiles in the same way that they might associate Sunderland with shipbuilding or Barnsley with coal. It was only when the traditional industries in these places were clearly disappearing that attempts were made to attract new ones. Ideally the time to set about encouraging substantial and enduring diversification would have been when such towns were booming. And when new concerns were attracted to Bradford in the post-war years their stay was often comparatively short. International Harvester, for instance, closed its factory in the early 1980s, only thirty years after it had opened. Baird TV opened a factory in Lidget Green in the early 1960s, but this closed down after less than twenty years, even though at one time it was producing 40 per cent of Britain's colour television sets. When it closed, as a result of foreign competition, 2,000 jobs were lost.

Newcomers

Paradoxically, although the textile industry was generally contracting in the post-war years, there was an acute labour shortage. Those manufacturers with any kind of vision realised that they would need to operate aggressively and at maximum capacity if they were to have any hope of remaining in business. This meant that, for the first time, some Bradford mills started to operate

twenty-four hours a day. Previously they had normally operated a day shift, with perhaps a short evening shift, staffed mainly by housewives for whom part-time work was convenient. As we have seen from earlier chapters, women had traditionally formed a substantial percentage of the workforce in Bradford's mills. The problem now was that many women, having experienced good wages and conditions in munitions factories and the like during the war, were reluctant to return to working in mills for low pay. For a time women were brought by bus from towns in south Yorkshire to work in Bradford, but this did not really solve the labour shortage. Legislation forbade women working nights in peacetime and many men did not want to have their lives disrupted by working the new nightshift. Families were beginning to realise too that in the new post-war world of educational opportunity, careers beyond the mills might now be available for their children.

How could this labour shortage be addressed? As luck would have it there were at the time thousands of people in displaced persons camps, mainly in Germany, who were only too willing to come to places like Bradford to start a new life. Many of these people were originally from countries that after the war were occupied by Stalin's Red Army and had thus become satellites of the USSR. Understandably, people were often reluctant to return to their places of origin if this was the case. A person's home might not even be in the same country as the one where he or she had lived before the war. Large parts of Poland, for example, were now in Ukraine and the Baltic states of Estonia, Latvia and Lithuania, independent countries before 1939, were now part of the USSR. So it was that thousands of newcomers came to work in Bradford's mills in the post-war period. The Poles and Ukrainians formed the largest groups, but there were also substantial numbers of people from Italy and Yugoslavia, with smaller numbers from Hungary, Byelorussia, Latvia and Estonia. They formed communities in the inner-city areas of Bradford at first, notably in Manningham and West Bowling, where housing was comparatively cheap. As time passed and they became more prosperous they often moved further from the city centre to more modern suburbs and the large housing estates built in the 1950s. Many of the Italians, some of whom had been prisoners of war, settled in Keighley.

The various communities set up their own support networks, their own churches and their own social clubs. The Latvians and Estonians, for example, acquired premises in Clifton Villas, off Manningham Lane, for their clubs and the Poles had clubs in Shearbridge Road and Edmund Street, where they also had their own Catholic church. By 1987 it was estimated that there were about

Polish Club, Edmund Street. (Sue Naylor)

4,000 inhabitants of Bradford with a Polish heritage, a similar number with a Ukrainian background and about 1,500 and 1,200 whose roots were in Italy and Yugoslavia respectively. Children from these communities attended local schools, and quickly became fluent in English and at ease with the English way of life. Lest they forget their roots, though, many were also sent to supplementary schools on a Saturday, where they learned the languages and imbibed the cultures of their original homelands.

More newcomers needed!

This influx of immigrants from eastern and central Europe eased the textile industry's labour shortage for a time, but by the late 1950s things began to change. On arrival the refugees had been happy to take any work that was going, but after a few years many of them began to look for better jobs than the textile mills could offer. Some had received a good education in their countries of origin and naturally they wanted, if possible, to put that to good use rather than spending their lives working as unskilled or semi-skilled employees. If that was impossible, they at least wanted their children to aspire to something better than mill work. A new source of inexpensive labour was required.

Immigrants from India and Pakistan began to arrive in Bradford from the mid-1950s onwards. In the early days it was groups of men who came, and most took up employment in the textile mills, usually on the nightshift. At first the numbers were comparatively small, but two factors led to many more immigrants coming to Bradford from the sub-continent.

The Mangla Dam is one of the largest in the world. It stands on the River Jhelum in the Mirpur district of Azad Kashmir, the part of the disputed territory of Kashmir that is administered by Pakistan. Construction started in 1961 and the dam was completed and became operational in 1967. Nearly 300 towns and villages in Mirpur and Dadyal districts were submerged because of the Mangla Dam and approximately 110,000 people were displaced and had to find new homes. The UK and Pakistan authorities made an agreement whereby those who wanted to come to Britain were granted work permits. Thousands took up the offer and many of these came to Bradford to find work.

At the same time as the Mangla Dam was being built the British Government passed the Immigration Act (1962). This was an attempt to control immigration by ending Britain's traditional open-door policy. One effect of the Act, perhaps unintended, was that it encouraged whole families, rather than just single

Hungarian Social Club, now closed. (Sue Naylor)

men, to migrate to Britain. The Asian immigrants of the 1950s fully expected to return to their homes once they had made some money in Bradford. Once the Mangla Dam was built it was clear that, for many, returning to their original homes was not an option. And once wives and children came, in the wake of the 1962 Act, it was equally clear that the Asian community would probably be in Bradford to stay. All well and good, except that before long the recession of the 1970s, exacerbated by the oil crisis of 1974, meant that there was no longer a labour shortage in Bradford – quite the reverse. In the 1970s more than 20,000 manufacturing jobs were lost, including about 16,000 in textiles and engineering. Newcomers who had come to work now found that they were at grave risk of being unemployed.

Like the Irish immigrants of the nineteenth century and the European immigrants of the post-war era, Bradford's Pakistani communities – mainly Mirpuris but with some Punjabis and Pashtuns – settled at first in inner-city areas, where housing was affordable and places of employment were close at hand. Initially the newcomers to Manningham lived in the streets around Lumb Lane, close to Drummond's Mill and in the Carlisle Road area, not far from Lister's Mill. Manningham had changed. The affluent residents of earlier years had moved away, and the large houses they had owned were now ideal for multiple occupancy or for converting into cheap flats. And there had always been plenty of working-class housing in Manningham too, so it was a natural port of entry for newcomers.

The years passed and families moved into other parts of the city, so that by the end of the twentieth century not just Manningham but the nearby sub-urbs of Girlington and Frizinghall were, in terms of ethnicity, predominantly British Asian, as were other localities, for example West Bowling, Little Horton and the Leeds Road area. As some Asian families became more affluent they moved to more salubrious suburbs, such as Heaton. Meanwhile, working-class white citizens occupied the large post-war council estates – Buttershaw, Holme Wood and Thorpe Edge – which had been built on the outskirts of the city. Many middle-class white families moved further out of Bradford to what had once been outlying villages, such as Clayton, Baildon or Wilsden, and these rapidly expanded into commuter communities.

The Pakistanis were not the only new arrivals. There was a Bangladeshi community in Bradford, most of whose members were originally from the remote Syhlet district of north-eastern Bangladesh. This was a smaller (and generally more impoverished) group than the Pakistanis. The Bangladeshis settled

A Bradford mosque. (Sue Naylor)

mainly in a neighbourhood on the lower side of Manningham Lane, close to Valley Parade football ground. Although the vast majority of Bradford's Asians were Muslims, a Hindu community took up residence in the lower part of Lidget Green, between Legrams Lane and Great Horton Road, and a Sikh community settled in part of Bradford Moor. In Keighley Pakistani families established themselves first in the Lawkholme Lane area of the town and later in the streets around Highfield Lane, while a smaller Bangladeshi community chose to live close to Lund Park.

The influx and development of these Asian communities had some parallels with the coming of the Irish immigrants to Bradford in the nineteenth century. In both cases the majority of people were moving from remote rural environments to a large industrial city in a foreign country where the indigenous people spoke another language and had a different religion. And in both cases the newcomers were initially obliged to take poorly paid employment and live in the poorest areas of the city. The Asian newcomers were met with some suspicion on the part of the host community at first, and even hostility at times, which was just what the Irish had experienced a century earlier.

It always takes time for new communities to become properly established, but eventually shops and businesses are opened and communities develop their own support mechanisms and infrastructure. As with the Irish and the

East Europeans, the Asians were particularly keen to set up their own places of worship. At first private houses were used for this. Later, larger buildings, no longer used for their original purposes, were taken over and adapted. The Elite Cinema on Toller Lane, for example, was converted into a mosque. By the end of the twentieth century several impressive purpose-built mosques had been built throughout the city and in Keighley, often in attractive local stone. The Sikh community had six gurudwaras by this time and early in the twenty-first century the Hindu community opened the Lakshmi Naranyan Temple. This, the largest Hindu temple in the North of England, was visited by the queen at the time of its opening.

Another sign that an erstwhile immigrant community is becoming well established is the entry of its members into the political arena. In 1985 Mohammed Ajeeb became the first man of Pakistani heritage to become the lord mayor of a British city and in 2011 Mrs Naveeda Ikram became the city's first Asian woman lord mayor. Marsha Singh, who had come to the city as a child, was elected MP for Bradford West in 1997. By the turn of the century the population of Bradford Metropolitan District as a whole was about 465,000, and 20 per cent of the inhabitants were estimated to be of Asian heritage, making that ethnic community one of the largest in the country.

Other newcomers arrived in Bradford. In 1987 there were an estimated 4,700 people in Bradford whose origins were in the West Indies (mainly the island of Dominica), and in the early 1980s a large group of Vietnamese boat-people came and were housed for a time in the buildings of the former Bingley College of Education. During the fighting in the former Yugoslavia in the 1990s refugees from Bosnia and Kosovo came, as did people fleeing conflicts in Sri Lanka and various countries in sub-Saharan Africa. In the early years of the twenty-first century, when the European Union expanded, there was another influx of people from eastern and central Europe – Poles and Slovaks in particular, including some Romani (or gipsy) families. In 2010, in view of its long history of welcoming people from all over the world, Bradford was, quite deservedly, given the status of City of Sanctuary.

Demolition and reconstruction

As noted in an earlier chapter Bradford escaped large-scale bombing in the Second World War, so there was no need to clear up wartime rubble once hos-

Asian clothes shop.
(Sue Naylor)

Polish shop. (Sue Naylor)

Probably the only Russian
restaurant in Yorkshire.
(Sue Naylor)

tilities had ceased. However, the Council was perhaps influenced by Nicholas Pevsner's rather unfair comment about the heart of Bradford: 'a small, mean and muddled city centre'. It is possibly true that the centre of Bradford, having grown piecemeal over the years, lacked formal grandeur and scale, but much of the impression of meanness most likely derived from the grimy appearance of the city-centre buildings. Years of smoke from scores of mill chimneys meant that nearly all of them were totally covered in black soot. The beauty of the buildings – those that were not demolished – would only become apparent years later when much of the stonework was cleaned and the mill chimneys that remained had ceased to belch forth their damaging and disfiguring smoke.

Soon after the war Stanley Wardley, the city engineer, devised an ambitious scheme that Bradford Council thought would improve matters. His master plan was put into operation in the early 1960s. It involved tearing down many of the Victorian buildings in the city centre and replacing them with edifices that were supposedly lighter in tone and – above all – more modern. At the time modernity was apparently all that mattered and the Council's planners seem to have had little regard for either the aesthetic or the historic importance of the buildings they were keen to demolish. For example, J.B. Priestley led a campaign to preserve Swan Arcade, but this did not succeed – and this impressive building was demolished in 1962 to be replaced with an uninspiring multi-storey office block. In fact the buildings that replaced the Victorian symbols of Bradford's prestige and prosperity, while certainly modern, were rarely of any merit. Local stone was replaced by large amounts of concrete or Portland stone, which quickly began to look discoloured and rather tired. Standing in a reconstructed Broadway, one of the city's main shopping streets, a person could well have been in any one of 100 identical pedestrianised precincts in towns and cities throughout Britain.

The climax to what some felt was a period of municipal vandalism came in 1972, when Kirkgate Market, a real gem of Victorian Bradford, was replaced by a quite repulsive concrete-clad shopping mall, in spite of protests from those citizens who could plainly see that the Council was dangerously close to throwing away the city's unique architectural heritage. Even when demolition did not occur some of Bradford's finest buildings, such as the Italianate warehouses in Little Germany, were hidden from view behind unattractive blocks of offices and shops. Years later, David Hockney expressed his view and was particularly prescient about the short life-span of the buildings Wardley had caused to be

built. Many of these had been demolished by the first decade of the twenty-first century: 'In the Sixties, when they pulled down Swan Arcade, most of the councillors wanted buildings that looked modern and that didn't cost much money. The idea is to make buildings very beautiful, but they said, "Oh that costs too much" and the consequence was very ugly buildings. It is wrong to economise on beauty because if you put up some thing awful it has to be pulled down in 20 years. It is false economy. It is far more economical to make things beautiful because they will be admired.'

When the Wool Exchange, possibly Bradford's most beautiful building, ceased to operate as a place for trading wool in the 1960s, a serious suggestion was made that it too should be demolished and replaced with something more in keeping with the modern *Zeitgeist*. For a time Salts Mill was considered ripe for demolition when textile production came to an end in the 1980s. Fortunately neither of these proposals came to anything, but they are a stark reminder of how a city's historical legacy can so easily be discarded. It was too late to save some historic houses that were located in Bradford's suburbs: Horton Hall and Bierley Hall were both pulled down at this time, though the oddly named Paper Hall in Barkerend Road, which was built in 1643 and had been derelict since the middle of the nineteenth century, managed to survive and in 1987 it was restored and put to a new use as office space.

In addition to erecting new buildings, Wardley sought to cater for the motorist by the construction of a dual-carriageway inner-ring road. The ring road was never totally completed, and all it really succeeded in doing was to constrict the city centre and create a quite formidable barrier between the main shopping streets and the area that contained the Alhambra Theatre, the Odeon Cinema, the Central Library and the University. Several pedestrian subways were constructed so that this busy road could be crossed, but people were nervous about using the gloomy passages, especially after dark, and when a heavy storm in the summer of 1968 caused the subways to flood it was feared for a time that people had drowned and frogmen were deployed to search for bodies.

A few years later Bradford obtained its own motorway, the M606, a 2 mile spur of the M62. The eighteenth-century leaders of Bradford had understood the importance of having a canal linking the town to a national waterways network and the M606 was a modern version of the same idea. While it did not perhaps extend far enough into the centre of the city, it did at least stimulate the growth of a trading estate – Euroway – along its margins, bringing some much-needed commercial activity to the city. Bradford's rail links, on the other hand, were neglected, and plans to stimulate the city's economy by linking the two rail termini, something which had been mooted as early as 1911, were shelved. Not far away Leeds was busily improving its railway provision and by the end of the century its impressive modern station had become one of the busiest in the country.

Bradford extends its boundaries

In 1974 local government throughout England was radically altered. In Yorkshire the old divisions, the three Ridings, which had existed since the Vikings settled in the North, were swept away. The textile towns and cities of the former West Riding now found themselves in the new county of West Yorkshire. Bradford became the principal partner in a newly created metropolitan district that stretched from the city itself almost to Skipton on the edge of the Yorkshire Dales and contained huge swathes of open countryside. Towns such as Keighley and Ilkley, which had relished their independence and individuality, were now subsumed into this new administrative unit, along with smaller places such as Denholme and Queensbury. The new district consisted of eleven former authorities in all.

The first issue to be faced was the choice of a name. Several bizarre suggestions were bandied about, including Wharfeaire, perhaps less a recognition of the two rivers flowing through the district than an acknowledgement of the hostility most of the smaller authorities felt towards Bradford, their much larger neighbour. Broadmoor was also suggested, presumably referring not to the beautiful countryside surrounding Bradford but to the criminal lunacy that some people felt had informed the whole reorganisation concept. Because it was impossible to arrive at a consensus locally, Whitehall civil servants had to make the final decision about the name, and thus the City of Bradford Metropolitan District came into being.

The chosen name naturally pleased people in Bradford itself, but it was hardly going to be popular elsewhere. For many years Shipley had managed to remain independent of Bradford, despite being so close to the city that a sharp eye was needed to spot where the administrative boundary between the two actually lay; now it seemed to the people of Shipley that their town had lost its identity and been swallowed up. The townspeople of Keighley were,

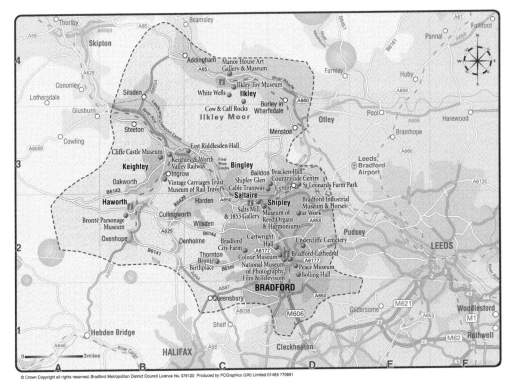

Map of the City of Bradford Metropolitan District after 1974, showing places of interest, as Bradford Council sought to promote Bradford as a tourist destination in the late twentieth century.

if possible, even more incensed. As an excepted district of the former West Riding, the town had had its own mayor and town council for years and a good deal of autonomy in matters such as school provision. Overnight this had gone. Few people in Keighley felt any affiliation with Bradford. For example, football fans were just as likely to give their allegiance to Leeds United or Burnley as to Bradford City FC.

The new Bradford Council had ninety members and the city (or Metropolitan District as it was officially known) had a new coat of arms, a peculiar hybrid made up of bits of the arms of the eleven former authorities. There was a new motto too, 'Progress, Industry, Humanity', which replaced Bradford's '*Labor Omnia Vincit*' (Work Conquers All). The new motto was rather bland, but at least it did not have its predecessor's unfortunate echo of '*Arbeit Macht Frei*'.

Some of the authorities had developed their own idiosyncratic ways of operating. In Denholme, for example, it had been customary for any vacant positions in the Council's small workforce to be advertised in a local fish-and-chip shop alongside notices about forthcoming jumble sales and lost pets. Such quaint practices had to go. The new regime favoured a modern corporate management approach, which from now on would emanate from the chief executive's office in the centre of Bradford. How effective the new arrangements would be in helping Bradford to face up to the challenges that were to come in the last part of the twentieth century and the early part of the twenty-first, nobody could tell.

thirteen

ARTISTS, WRITERS AND SCIENTISTS

As we have seen in Chapter Five, Bradford's German community produced its share of notables in the various arts, but over the years there have been other people, born in Bradford, who have achieved international fame in a variety of artistic and scientific fields. One obtained a Nobel Prize, another wrote one of the greatest works of fiction in the English language and one produced a theory about the origins of the universe that was widely accepted for much of the twentieth century. Most of the people whose lives and work are described in this chapter came to prominence after they had left the area, but they were all born and raised in or near to the city, so their lives form part of the story of Bradford. We start with two writers.

Emily Brontë (1818-48)

Virginia Woolf was an admirer of the Brontë sisters and after she visited Haworth in 1904 she described how she felt their work was shaped by their environment: 'Haworth expresses the Brontës; the Brontës express Haworth; they fit like a snail to its shell.'

One of the Brontë sisters, Emily, is something of an enigma. Unlike her sister Charlotte and her brother Branwell, she never sought fame and she remained unknown to the general public during her short life, yet *Wuthering Heights* is usually regarded as one of the finest English novels ever written. Branwell, who erroneously imagined that he was a talented artist, failed in his quest for fame and descended into alcoholism and opium abuse. Charlotte achieved fame after *Jane Eyre* was published and she went on to mix with prominent figures in the literary establishment of the day.

By contrast Emily was a recluse. She was born in Thornton, where her father, Patrick – originally from Ireland – was the local vicar. In the early 1820s the

Brontë Parsonage, Haworth. (Sue Naylor)

family moved to Haworth, where Patrick had obtained the position of perpet-
ual curate. Whether at the Clergy Daughters School at Cowan Bridge, or at
Miss Wooler's School at Roe Head, or at the Pensionnat Heger in Brussels – all
places she attended as part of her education – Emily was constantly homesick
to the point of being physically ill. Career opportunities for women of her class,
even those with some education, were virtually non-existent; teaching or working as a governess were really the only possibilities. Unlike her sisters, Emily
never worked as a governess and only worked as a teacher for a few months at
Miss Patchett's School, near Halifax, and for a brief period at the Pensionnat
Heger. The rest of her life was spent in Haworth, undertaking household duties
at the parsonage, walking on the nearby moors – and secretly writing.

As children, Emily and her sisters and brother wrote stories and poems
about two imaginary countries, Angria and Gondal. This was perhaps an under-
standable form of escapism, given that their mother was dead, their father
was austere and remote (he took his meals alone) and their lives were circum-
scribed by Haworth, which at that time was a rough and ready industrial boom
town, surrounded by inhospitable countryside. Emily probably started to write
Wuthering Heights in 1845. About the same time Charlotte came across some of
Emily's poems. Although angry at first that her writings had been discovered,
Emily was eventually persuaded to join with Charlotte and Anne in the production of a volume of poetry, which was published at the sisters' own expense.

It is said that only two copies were sold. The sisters had adopted men's names in their attempt to get their poems published and Emily retained hers – Ellis Bell – when she submitted *Wuthering Heights* for publication. Published in 1847, this was her only novel, although she may have been working on another when she died the following year. The manuscript of this second book has never been found, but there is a legend that it is buried somewhere in the garden of Haworth Parsonage.

Wuthering Heights, though possibly less well known (and often less well understood) than Charlotte's *Jane Eyre*, is now regarded as the superior work. It met with mixed reviews when it was first published, principally because many reviewers found it shocking and unclassifiable. The more conventional *Jane Eyre* was an almost instant success. Readers could readily understand the rather melodramatic plot and Charlotte's hero and heroine, Rochester and Jane, act in ways that are never puzzling or too upsetting. They are fundamentally sympathetic characters. This is certainly not the case with Heathcliff and Cathy, the two protagonists of *Wuthering Heights*. Cathy is selfish, self-delusional and immature; Heathcliff is a vindictive monster – probably a murderer and perhaps even a necrophiliac. The pair's *folie à deux* makes them totally unlike any other hero and heroine in literature, with the possible exception of Macbeth and Lady Macbeth. One must speculate that the makers of some films based on the book, especially the 1939 Hollywood version, starring Laurence Olivier and Merle Oberon, had not read the book carefully enough to understand what Emily was actually writing about. And as for Cliff Richard's musical version and Kate Bush's 1970s pop song, the less said the better.

Emily Brontë was a genius; her sisters Anne and Charlotte were both talented writers. All three were products of the Bradford area and were inspired by its landscapes and its communities.

John Braine (1922-86)

In *Memoirs* (1991) Kingsley Amis wrote the following about his friend, John Braine: 'his dream of real success was of a triumphal procession through Bradford with himself at the head, flanked by a pair of naked beauties draped with jewellery'.

Braine was born near to St Patrick's Church in Sedgefield Terrace in what had been an area of Bradford populated by Irish immigrants in the nineteenth century (see Chapter Five). His mother was of Irish descent and Braine was educated at St Bede's Catholic Grammar School. He left school at the age of sixteen and had a variety of jobs before qualifying as a librarian, eventually working for eleven years at Bingley Library. He looked upon his time in Bingley as the period when he educated himself, but all the while he was apparently dreaming of somehow escaping from what he considered to be a constricting provincial existence. His first version of *Room at the Top* was submitted to publishers in 1951, but was rejected. Braine became ill with tuberculosis a little later and it was during his convalescence in a sanatorium near Grassington that he re-wrote the book. It was published in 1957 and became an overnight sensation and a bestseller. Between 1959 and his death he wrote another dozen or so books, but none had anything like the impact (or indeed the quality) of *Room at the Top*.

Room at the Top is particularly important because of the way it describes the underlying tensions within English society in the immediate post-war period. People were aware that some things had changed quite profoundly because of the war and because of the policies of Atlee's Labour Government, but at the same time there was a sense that the old social order was still there and not about to give way. This is perhaps best summed up by a line in John Osborne's ground-breaking play of 1957, *Look Back in Anger*. The character Alison compares the feelings of her traditionally-minded father, Colonel Redfern, with those of her rebellious husband, Jimmy Porter: 'You're hurt because everything is changed. Jimmy is hurt because everything is the same.'

The hero of *Room at the Top,* Joe Lampton believes, just like Jimmy Porter, that things have not really changed in England. There is no real equality of opportunity and so there is only one way for him, a bright but penniless product of the working-class, to get to the top; by cynically exploiting every opportunity, including marrying the daughter of a wealthy local industrialist after getting her pregnant. However, Joe is fully aware that he has made a Faustian pact – marrying someone he does not love in order to gain the social position and wealth that he desires. He pays a heavy price for his entry to a privileged class.

Braine's book led to him being categorised as an Angry Young Man, along with Osborne and other authors, such as Kingsley Amis and John Wain. These writers were initially left wing politically and wished to draw attention to what they considered to be the social injustices prevailing in England. Ironically most of the group, including Braine, moved to the far right in their politics as they got older. Braine even wrote a pamphlet for the right-wing Monday Club

in the mid-1960s, called *Goodbye to the Left*. He ended up as a supporter of the apartheid regime in South Africa and welcomed America's escalation of the war in Vietnam. Sadly he also ended up living alone and over-dependent on alcohol after his marriage broke down.

Braine said that Bingley was the town he had in mind as the setting for *Room at the Top*, but when a film of the book was made in 1959 most of the location shots were taken in Halifax and in the centre of Bradford. In one scene Laurence Harvey (somewhat miscast as Joe) and Simone Signoret (who won an Oscar for playing Alice, the woman Joe really loves) are seen drinking in the Boy and Barrel pub in Westgate. Other films were shot in Bradford in the 1960s, notably a version of Keith Waterhouse's novel *Billy Liar,* and since then film and television companies have frequently used the city as a location. For example, Alan Bennett's *The Insurance Man*, a film made in 1985 about Franz Kafka, used the warehouse area of Little Germany to convincing effect to depict Prague. Frequent film and the presence of the National Media Museum in the city led, in 2009, to Bradford being designated the first official UNESCO City of Film.

As for John Braine, once he left Bradford to live in Surrey he never wrote much that is worth reading. Perhaps moving away from his roots made him a victim of the very thing he spoke of in a BBC television programme, broadcast in 1971: 'To become an expatriate is to remove oneself from the source of one's nourishment.'

David Hockney (b. 1937)

Hockney is Britain's best known contemporary artist and he has an international reputation. Born in Bradford and brought up in Eccleshill, he was educated at Bradford Grammar School. During his time there he made sure that his school work was never bad enough for him to be thrown out altogether but never good enough for him to be promoted out of the bottom form, for it was only in the bottom form that boys could study art. Bradford Grammar School had a tradition of academic excellence, but it also subscribed to the peculiarly English notion that art as a school subject was only for those who were not really up to studying supposedly more important subjects, such as classics or the sciences.

Hockney has said that as a child, soon after the Second World War, he would watch his father renovating secondhand bicycles to sell. At that time new bicycles were hard to come by as most went for export. What particularly fascinated Hockney was the way his father's brush applied the thick paint to the metal frames of the bicycles. Even as an adult Hockney says he could always derive great pleasure from the simple but sensual act of painting something like the flat surface of a door in one colour.

After leaving Bradford Grammar School Hockney attended Bradford Art College. Much of a student's time there involved concentrating on traditional figure drawing, something that Hockney came to value greatly because it gave a solid foundation to his developing technique. It was here too that he sold his first picture, a portrait of his father. He received £10 for it, but a portion of this had to be used, in accordance with the custom, to buy a round of drinks for his fellow students in the Mannville Arms, the pub next door to the Art College. Hockney may also have painted some murals to decorate the walls of the nearby Alassio coffee bar, a favourite haunt of Bradford's art students and bohemians at that time. The Alassio was later pulled down to make way for a new police station, so it is possible that some Hockney originals, which would now be worth a phenomenal amount of money, were thrown into a demolition contractor's skip.

Hockney left Bradford to study at the Royal College of Art, where his reputation as a highly talented and innovative artist started to develop. In 1964 he moved to the USA and his reputation grew further. His series of paintings featuring Californian swimming pools became internationally famous and in 1974 one of them, *A Bigger Splash*, provided the title for a film about Hockney's life and work.

In the later part of the twentieth century Hockney started to produce photo collages – what he called 'joiners' – and he also made much use of fax machines, digital cameras and other technological equipment to produce his art. Works by him are in galleries throughout the world. Despite living in America for many years and later in East Yorkshire, Hockney has always maintained his connection with Bradford. Salts Mill contains a gallery that houses an impressive collection of his work. In January 2012 Hockney was awarded the Order of Merit, having previously declined a knighthood.

Edward Appleton (1892-1965)

Appleton was born and spent his early life in Bradford, attending Hanson School before going on to Cambridge University. He served with the Royal Engineers in the First World War and it was at this time that he began to develop an interest in radio. After the war he returned to academic life and in 1924 he became Professor of Physics at King's College, London. From 1936 to 1939 he was Professor of Natural Philosophy at Cambridge.

At London and at Cambridge he researched further into the field of radio and was particularly interested in the question of why radio waves behave in one way during daylight and in a different way after dark. Using BBC transmitters he was able to confirm that radio waves were reflected back to earth by a heavily ionised layer – the ionosphere – in the upper atmosphere and that this layer was subject to changes caused by the presence or absence of sunlight. The existence of such a layer had been correctly postulated as early as 1902 by Oliver Heaviside and A.E. Kennelly, but Appleton's work went further. He successfully identified a sub-division of the ionosphere, which became known as the Appleton layer. This was about 210 miles above the earth and was the first object ever to have been discovered solely by radio. Short-wave radio signals could be reflected from the Appleton layer and this opened up the possibility of round-the-world broadcasting.

One aspect of Appleton's research was to become vital during the Second World War. In 1939 he became Secretary of the Department of Scientific and Industrial Research – the British Government's senior post relating to physics. In this role he advised the government, among other things, that the development of an atomic bomb was feasible, but his real claim to fame came from another source. By now his work on radio waves had progressed further, and paved the way for Robert Watson-Watt and his team to develop radar.

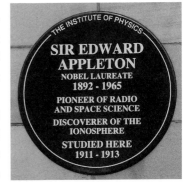

Plaque commemorating Edward Appleton at Bradford University. (Sue Naylor)

Britain was threatened with invasion in 1940 after the collapse of France. It is usually agreed that the victory of the RAF over the Luftwaffe in the Battle of Britain was crucial in forestalling the invasion threat; and it is also generally agreed that the use of radar was the single most important factor in the RAF's success, for it enabled British fighter aircraft to be deployed quickly and effectively to attack German planes approaching Britain. Without radar the Battle of Britain would probably have been lost and Britain might well have been successfully invaded and occupied by the Nazis. Without Appleton's pioneering work with radio waves there would have been no radar.

The British people owed Appleton a debt of gratitude and in 1941 he was knighted. Other honours followed and in 1947 he was awarded the Nobel Prize in physics for his work. Two years later he became the principal and vice-chancellor of Edinburgh University, a position he held until his death in 1965. Appleton is well remembered in Bradford. In 2009 a new secondary school, Appleton Academy, named in his honour, was opened in Wyke, in the south of the city.

Fred Hoyle (1915-2001)

After much discussion and some protests by environmentalists a bypass was built in the early twenty-first century to alleviate traffic congestion in the centre of Bingley. A few years later the bypass was named Sir Fred Hoyle Way as a tribute to one of the most esteemed English scientists of the twentieth century. Hoyle was born in Bingley, his family home in Primrose Lane, which winds downhill from Gilstead to the Leeds and Liverpool Canal. Throughout his life Hoyle courted controversy and was frequently outspoken. This characteristic apparently started at an early age, for he would often refuse to go to his infants school on the grounds that he could learn more without the interference of teachers; throughout his life he never suffered fools gladly. Once he was at Bingley Grammar School he became for a time more compliant and in due course he gained a place at Cambridge to study mathematics. He had also become deeply interested in astronomy and his subsequent academic career was mainly concerned with astronomy, physics and evolution.

Hoyle is known best for rejecting the so-called Big Bang theory of the origin of the universe in favour of his own steady-state theory, which proposed that the universe has always existed. He acknowledged that the universe was expanding, as others had said, but he theorised that as the galaxies got further apart others developed to fill the space. The analogy Hoyle used to explain this to the non-specialist was that of a river – the individual water molecules move on but the overall river itself remains. He also developed a theory that the chemical elements could have their origin in the hot interiors of stars. Many of his colleagues in the scientific fraternity believed that he should have received a Nobel Prize for his work in this area.

In 1958 Hoyle became Professor of Astrophysics and Natural Philosophy at Cambridge University and in 1966 he founded the Institute of Theoretical Astronomy. However, his forthrightness led to clashes with some members of the university's hierarchy and in 1972 he resigned his professorship and the chairmanship of the Institute. After that he was able to pursue his work free of any unnecessary interference. From 1969 to 1971 he was vice-president of the Royal Society. In 1972 he was knighted.

Hoyle was an excellent communicator and keen to keep the general public informed about scientific issues, rather than these being solely the preserve of an exclusive elite of scientists. Thus he made several radio broadcasts in the 1950s about astronomy and he wrote popular scientific books, such as *The Nature of the Universe*. Although he started out as a confirmed atheist, his researches led him to reconsider his views and in a 1982 lecture, entitled *Evolution from Space*, he made the following statement: 'one arrives at the conclusion that biomaterials with their amazing measure or order must be the outcome of intelligent design'. Mainstream evolutionary biologists referred to his view as Hoyle's Fallacy, especially when he went further and developed his theory that life on earth had evolved because of influxes of viruses delivered by meteors. He even went so far as to suggest that periodic influenza epidemics were a result of the earth passing through certain meteor streams. Despite opposition (and some scorn), Hoyle stuck to his views.

Many of Hoyle's pronouncements have an air of science-fiction about them, so it is not surprising that as well as his academic writings and his popular scientific works he wrote over a dozen science-fiction novels, of which *The Black Cloud*, published in the late 1950s, is probably the best known. *A for Andromeda*, which came out in the early 1960s, was also well received, and later there was a television adaptation of the book.

When Fred Hoyle died in 2001 many tributes were paid to a man who from childhood was always going to do things his own way, irrespective of the views of others. He contributed a considerable amount to the major scientific debates of the twentieth century. In an obituary in the *Independent* C. Wickramasingh said this of him: 'Hoyle sought to answer some of the biggest questions in science. How did the universe originate? How did life begin? What are the eventual fates of the planets, stars and galaxies?'

Joseph Wright (1855-1930)

Joseph Wright's life story has something of the fairytale about it. He was born in Thackley of poor parents and at the age of six was working in a local quarry in charge of a donkey cart. Later he worked at Salts Mill as a doffer, whose job – one of the lowliest in a textile mill – was to replace full bobbins with empty ones in the spinning department. Eventually he was promoted to wool-sorter at £1 per week. Salts Mill had a factory school for its child workers and Wright attended it, but he was scarcely literate even at the age of fifteen. In order to remedy this he taught himself to read by studying the Bible and Bunyan's *Pilgrim's Progress*.

He became fascinated by language and now that he had gained some mastery of written English he set about learning French, German and Latin in the evenings at Bradford's Mechanics Institute. He earned some money to pay the fees by setting up his own night-school class to teach other boys who, like himself, had lacked the opportunity to receive much education. By 1876 he had accumulated £40 with which he went to study for one term at the prestigious University of Heidelberg in Germany. In order to economise he walked from Antwerp to Heidelberg. On his return to England he enrolled at the Yorkshire College of Science (now Leeds University), supporting himself by teaching and in 1885 he returned to Heidelberg to complete a PhD.

Wright returned to England once again in 1888. At that time Max Müller was Professor of Philology at Oxford University. He was the most eminent philologist in Europe and he had heard of the remarkable Wright from colleagues at Heidelberg. As a result he appointed Wright as his deputy. At first the dons at Oxford believed that Wright's appointment was some kind of joke – how could this man, from such an impoverished background and speaking in a broad Bradford accent, possibly have been elevated to such a position? But Müller was not English, so the social snobbery characteristic of Oxford in those days did not influence him. He knew that Wright's academic brilliance, not his origins or mode of speech, was what counted.

Wright enjoyed great success as a teacher and a scholar. In 1901 he became Professor of Philology at Oxford and held the post until he retired in 1925. He specialised in Germanic languages but was also deeply interested in English dialects. He published the *Windhill Dialect Grammar* in 1893, which again was initially regarded by some as a practical joke, for why would anyone spend time researching the language of a small and unknown community between Shipley and Bradford? But this was only the start. Between 1895 and 1905 Wright, assisted by his wife Elizabeth, produced his *English Dialect Dictionary* in six volumes – regarded even today as the definitive work on dialects.

At one stage Wright was tutor to J.R.R. Tolkien, the author of *Lord of the Rings*, and greatly influenced him regarding the study of language (Wright himself had command of at least fifteen). Virginia Woolf admired Wright's work, as did Thomas Hardy. The house that Elizabeth and Joseph lived in for many years in Oxford was named Thackley, after Wright's birthplace, and a feature of their social lives was giving hospitality to students on Sundays in the form of traditional Yorkshire teas. Joseph Wright was a very remarkable man with a formidable intellect and a massive capacity for rigorous, scholarly work.

J.B. Priestley (1894-1984)

Priestley was born at 34 Mannheim Road in Manningham and grew up at 5 Saltburn Place, just a few hundred yards away. He was educated at Belle Vue Boys' School and afterwards worked for a firm of wool merchants – something he found extremely irksome. He was wounded in the First World War and when he was discharged from the army he went to Cambridge University, graduating in 1921 with a degree in history and political science. Although he frequently returned to Bradford in the years that followed, he never again lived in the city.

From an early age Priestley was determined to be a writer and after the publication in 1929 of his novel *The Good Companions* he became famous. However, he was somewhat disdainful of the attention lavished on this bestseller and always considered that *Bright Day* (1946) and *Angel Pavement* (1930) were superior works. He wrote about thirty novels in all and numerous stage plays. The plays have, in general, endured better than the novels and *When We Are Married* has remained a favourite, especially with amateur theatre companies, into the twenty-first century. *An Inspector Calls* has also been frequently revived. One theme of this play is the nature of

Statue of JB Priestley. (Sue Naylor)

time, something that greatly interested Priestley and something he explored in other plays, notably *Time and the Conways* and *I Have Been Here Before*.

During the early part of the Second World War Priestley made a series of Sunday night broadcasts for BBC radio entitled *Postscript*. These were hugely popular and at the time only Churchill himself was able to draw a larger radio audience. However, complaints were made in some quarters that Priestley was espousing socialism (as well as speaking in a Yorkshire accent), so he was taken off the air. He never made a secret of his left-wing political views, and his plays frequently criticise the snobbery and injustice to which he felt English society was particularly prone.

While Priestley enjoyed widespread popularity in Britain and abroad, his relationship with his native city was, especially in the 1950s and 1960s, not an easy one. Some people in Bradford felt that he had turned his back on the city, which in some ways he had. On the other hand he frequently wrote about the city, and fictionalised it as Bruddersford in more than one book. But things came to a head in 1958 when he made a BBC television documentary entitled *Lost City*. There was outrage in the correspondence columns of the local press; many people felt that not only had he deserted Bradford but he was also condemning it. Priestley defended himself by stating that the title was a nostalgic reference to the Bradford of his youth and was not meant to be a negative comment on the modern city. Few in Bradford were convinced. Eventually, however, some kind of harmony was restored and in 1973 Priestley was granted the freedom of the city. The *Telegraph and Argus* commented at the time: 'Yorkshiremen, of all people, should be able to forgive a man for being blunt. J.B. Priestley's bluntness has obviously delayed, for many years, the decision to bestow on him the Freedom of Bradford. However, Bradford has now decided, if somewhat belatedly, to embrace its most famous son, warts and all. He is delighted by this one honour which he obviously desired above all others.'

FIRES AND DISTURBANCES

A city that contains scores of warehouses, most of them built in Victorian times, some disused, others containing highly inflammable textiles, is going to have more than its share of fires. Hardly a year went by, especially in the later decades of the twentieth century, without there being several major conflagrations in Bradford. Not all of them involved textile warehouses. In 1979, for example, the once-fashionable Busbys department store on Manningham Lane (re-christened as a branch of Debenhams by then) was totally destroyed by a spectacular blaze, as in other years were Eastbrook Hall, Bradford Playhouse and Film Theatre (twice in seventy years) and several schools. Of course the cynics said that many of the warehouse fires were deliberately started so that insurance money could be collected by the owners of firms that were in terminal decline and certainly there was evidence that, in the case of some fires in empty or derelict textile premises, arsonists had been at work.

However, the two fires described in this chapter did not involve warehouses. One was the tragic Bradford City fire at Valley Parade in May 1985, at which fifty-six people died. The other fire was much smaller and took place in January 1989 outside City Hall. Nobody died on that occasion and the only thing that was destroyed was one book.

Death at Valley Parade, 11 May 1985

Bradford City football club was founded in 1908, and some might say that like many things in Bradford its best days were in the years before 1914. In 1911 the club beat Newcastle United to win the FA Cup, which coincidentally was a brand-new trophy, manufactured by the Bradford-based Fattorini firm of jewellers to replace the original cup, which had been stolen. Since those glory days

Bradford City Fire Memorial. (Photography by Dan Grant)

the club had usually languished in the lower divisions of the Football League, but at least it still existed in the 1980s, unlike its rival club, Bradford Park Avenue, which had dropped out of the Football League altogether in 1970 and gone into liquidation in 1974. In fact Bradford City too almost went out of existence in 1983 because of financial difficulties, but it was rescued by a new board of directors who bought the club for a very modest £40,000. The club's supporters raised a similar amount to pay the players' wages, and Bradford Council agreed to a mortgage on the club's Valley Parade ground of £100,000. The club was saved.

Two seasons later Bradford City were Division Three champions and had secured promotion to Division Two of the Football League. Their final match that season was on 11 May 1985 against Lincoln City. With the championship already assured, this fixture should have been something of a celebration of the club's success that season. Instead it turned into a tragedy.

Few people who attended the match could afterwards remember much about the first half of the game, but nobody would ever forget what happened just before half-time. The Valley Parade ground was old and in serious need of repair. The main stand was a wooden construction and – ironically – was due to be replaced by something more modern during the close season that year: the steel for a new roof had already been delivered. In the closing minutes of the first half a small fire broke out between two rows of seats near one end of the stand. It is likely that accumulated litter beneath the wooden flooring of the stand was accidentally ignited by a discarded cigarette or match. At first nobody took much notice and play continued, but very soon the flames began to grow and spread. Police officers entered the stand and urged spectators to leave their seats and seek safety by coming onto the pitch. But many people's natural reaction was to go the other way – after all, only hooligans invaded football pitches – so they headed for the exits at the rear of the stand. This was the worst thing they could have done, for most of the exit doors were locked and there were no stewards present to unlock them. After a frighteningly short time the whole of the stand was engulfed in smoke and flames. Many people were trapped and died in the area close to the locked exits.

The roof of the stand was made from wooden rafters covered with asphalt and when it caught fire, scarcely a minute later, a fireball raced through the whole of the stand and the temperature rose to an estimated 900°C. As a result synthetic clothing – hats, gloves, coats – was welded onto people's flesh. Some bodies were later found still in their seats, burned to death by molten debris that had dropped onto them from the roof. People scrambled over the rather high perimeter wall between the stand and the pitch with their hair on fire, and the police officers assisting them found that the plastic peaks of their caps started to melt. The grass along the touchline near the stand began to burn. By this time the referee had led the players from the field, and the 4,000 or so people who had only minutes previously been sitting in the stand, watching a rather dull game of football, were soon all on the pitch, many badly burned – either that or they were among the fifty-six who perished in the dreadful fire.

It is a cliché that terrible events often bring out the best in people. Spectators as well as police officers performed deeds of great bravery and not a few suffered severe burns through assisting others to get to safety, some returning more than once to the perimeter wall to help people get onto the pitch. Four policemen and two spectators were awarded the Queen's Gallantry Medal

Bradford City's new stand at Valley Parade. (Photography by Dan Grant)

for their courageous and selfless behaviour that afternoon. In all twenty-eight police officers and twenty-two spectators were publicly documented as having saved at least one life. A little later many Bangladeshi families who lived near to Valley Parade opened their doors and provided tea and comfort to shocked spectators trudging away from the ground, where by now the fire brigade was trying to get the blaze under control.

In the following months almost £4 million was raised for a disaster fund, to which people from all over the world contributed. The queen sent a message of condolence to the city. Prime Minister Margaret Thatcher turned up to offer solace to the citizens of Bradford. The owner of the *Daily Mirror*, Robert Maxwell, also came, but he was only really interested in a story about who might be to blame for the fire and loss of life. Nobody was, as the subsequent official enquiry firmly established. An interim report was published in July 1985, and in his summing-up Oliver Popplewell, who chaired the enquiry, made the following statement:

> Comparing the reaction of those involved in the Bradford disaster with those involved in some other disasters, one can only be astonished at the wonderful way that the citizens of Bradford behaved. They quietly buried their dead, tended their injured and comforted their bereaved. They did not pursue seemingly endless inquiries as a personal vendetta. They did not seek to use their disaster as a weapon of emotional blackmail on the government, nor did they seek to perpetuate publicly the memory of the terrible disaster they had suffered. They behaved with great dignity and no little courage.

Burning *The Satanic Verses*, 14 January 1989

Salman Rushdie had already won the Booker Prize for *Midnight's Children* in 1981 and he was regarded as one of the most important writers of English fiction when *The Satanic Verses* was published in 1988. The book won the Whitbread Award that year and nearly won its author a second Booker Prize. But rather than presenting Rushdie with awards and prizes, Muslims throughout the world, especially in the Indian sub-continent, protested that his book was grossly insulting to Islam and highly offensive to them. Violent demonstrations against the book led to people being killed in India and a total of fifty countries banned it.

Leaders of Bradford's Muslim community joined the protest, demanding that the book be banned, that the English blasphemy laws be extended to cover all religions, not just Christianity, and that there should be an apology from Rushdie for writing something so offensive. There was scant response to these demands from the book's publisher or from the MPs who were approached, although some Bradford bookshops did remove the book from display. Something else had to be done to show the Muslim community's profound disapproval. On 14 January 1989 a large group gathered in the Tyrls, between the magistrates' court and City Hall, in order to make their protest about *The Satanic Verses*.

One must bear in mind that throughout the rather turbulent 1980s the authorities in Bradford were quite used to protests being held near to City Hall or in some cases inside the building itself. There had, for instance, been demonstrations protesting about a proposed 30 per cent increase in the rates, and other protests about the swingeing cuts in municipal services that the Leader of the Council, Eric Pickles (later to be a senior minister in David Cameron's cabinet), was intent on implementing. There were protests too about halal food in school canteens and about Ray Honeyford's position as headteacher of Drummond Middle School (see Chapter fifteen). There had even been a demonstration to protest about the possible demise of Bradford City football club. It is likely, therefore, that a conventional demonstration against *The Satanic Verses* would have passed almost unnoticed in the city. After all, the protest was peaceful enough. But it involved a book burning – and that made all the difference.

In the *BBC News Magazine* (13 February 2009) Ishtiaq Ahmed of the Bradford Council of Mosques recalled the rationale of the protest as follows: 'A spot was selected – it had a symbolic meaning ... a faith community demonstrating and saying "We matter, we exist, we are here, our presence matters. This police station, town hall, magistrates' court are ours as much as anyone else's" ... People became more aware about the presence of Muslims, more aware of their sensibilities regarding their faith.' Indeed they did. The problem was that while the burning of a book might be an accepted feature of protests in other parts of the world, in Europe it has a particular resonance. It is unequivocally associated with the book-burnings carried out in Nazi Germany, and that resonance was made all the more painful in Bradford because so many of its citizens were descendants of families that had been brutally treated and in many cases destroyed by the Nazi regime. For these people the words of the German poet Heinrich Heine (1797-1856) were particularly important: 'Where one burns books one will, in the end, burn people.'

Images of the Bradford book-burning went around the globe. Exactly one month after the event Ayatollah Khomeini issued his fatwa, stating that it was the sacred duty of all devout Muslims to kill Salman Rushdie if they got the chance. It has been said that the fatwa had less to do with religious matters than political ones, that it was really just a ploy to gain more support for the Iranian regime at home and abroad. Be that as it may, Rushdie, fearing for his life, went into hiding for the next ten years.

The burning of the book, followed so quickly by the issuing of the fatwa, constituted a major turning point in Bradford, for it threatened to create new divisions between the Muslim community and the rest of the populace, just at a time when some observers felt that community relations in the city might be improving. Certainly, as Ishtiaq Ahmed said, people were made more aware of the sensibilities of Muslims, but it was also clear that people who had for years been stoically passive in the face of hostility and humiliation were now much more likely to stand up for themselves. Nobody knew what the ramifications of that would be.

The Manningham disturbances, 9-11 June 1995

Ostensibly the cause of the so-called Manningham disturbances in June 1995 was heavy-handed police intervention in a domestic incident at an address close to Oak Lane, one of the main thoroughfares running through Manningham. Some arrests were made, but rumours spread quickly that the police had assaulted a pregnant woman and soon there was even a wild story that a baby had been killed. Before long a large crowd had gathered in front of Lawcroft House, the police station on Lilycroft Road, to demand the release of those arrested. Built at a cost of £7 million, Lawcroft House presented an image that was the antithesis of neighbourhood community policing. With its massive walls and forbidding appearance, it looked very like a fortress that an occupying power might have constructed in hostile territory to subdue the local populace – certainly more Robocop than Dixon of Dock Green.

Those arrested were not released, and police officers in riot gear were deployed to confront the increasingly angry crowd. Some windows in nearby shops were smashed and a fire was lit where Oak Lane meets St Mary's Road,

View of where the 1995 disturbances occurred in Oak Lane, Manningham. (Sue Naylor)

but at this point there was no indication that things would escalate into a major incident. The next day some of the shopkeepers in Oak Lane put protective boards over their windows and there were rumours – totally without foundation – that the National Front was going to show up. Nothing of significance happened until the evening. At about eight o'clock the police, in full riot gear, formed a line in Oak Lane to face a group of about 150 young Asian men who began to hurl stones and later petrol bombs at them. This went on for some time, until a little before nine o'clock the police suddenly and inexplicably withdrew. This encouraged the mob to set off down Oak Lane, turn right into Manningham Lane and head towards the city centre. Bradford lay before them, an open and undefended city.

The next day (a Sunday) it was perfectly easy to trace the route the mob had taken, because the streets and pavements were full of broken glass. If the burning of *The Satanic Verses* six years earlier had evoked memories of Nazi book-burnings, the scene on that Sunday morning was now reminiscent of *Kristallnacht* in 1938, when Nazi storm troopers had gone on the rampage against Jewish synagogues and shops throughout Germany.

The Manningham disturbances caused about £1 million of damage, but very few arrests were made and those were for minor offences. In all thirty-three Bradford businesses were attacked; as a consequence some moved away from Bradford altogether and others relocated to premises well away from Manningham. For a time many of the excellent curry houses in and around Oak Lane suffered because their usual non-Asian customers were too nervous to come into the area. The Manningham disturbances were bad for business, not just in Manningham but in Bradford as a whole.

Because the Home Secretary refused to sanction a judicial enquiry, a local commission was set up to investigate the causes of the disturbances. Three commissioners were appointed to collect evidence and views from a wide range of people and then produce a report on their findings. In keeping perhaps with long-standing Bradford traditions, the commissioners could not agree, so two separate reports were eventually published. However, there was consensus on some points, notably that Bradford Council lacked a coherent approach to dealing with the complex issues that had rapidly overtaken the city towards the end of the twentieth century – as the Bradford Commission Report (1996) made clear: 'When the Commission wanted to know what problems, in the area the disorders began, had been identified, and what measured progress was being achieved in meeting these problems, we had to discuss our interest with what seemed like 57 Varieties of organisations, each separately dedicated to meeting those problems. Bradford currently lacks a capacity to sort out the wood from the trees ...'

Blaming Bradford Council was perhaps too easy; the reality was that nobody knew what to do for the best. The government's rather simplistic approach was to throw money at the problem, so the Single Regeneration Budget (SRB) was deployed. This provided capital funding for the refurbishment of school buildings in the Manningham area and for grants to enable owner-occupiers to improve their homes. It also provided cash to encourage the recruitment of more police officers from ethnic communities. Small-scale projects to provide additional educational resources, such as homework clubs, were also funded. The money was welcome, but whether these measures really addressed the root causes of the disturbances nobody could tell, because nobody really knew what those root causes were. Some cited racism; others poverty or unemployment, social deprivation or a lack of education. Some said that the young men of Manningham, Bradford-born Asians, had become a law unto themselves – alienated from their parents and elders, whose values and lifestyle were still rooted in Pakistan. In truth the only thing most people agreed on was the likelihood of something similar happening again in Bradford before too long.

The Bradford riots, 7-8 July 2001

Whereas the events of June 1995 had been declared to be merely 'disturbances', there was no doubt that the much more serious events of July 2001 could only be described as riots. Indeed they were reckoned to be the worst riots on the British mainland for many years.

There had already been confrontations between white and Asian youths in Oldham and Burnley that summer and the British National Party (BNP) was campaigning in both towns, intending to field candidates in the general election. The BNP planned a rally in Bradford to coincide with the final day of the Bradford Festival and the Anti-Nazi League (ANL) intended to hold a counter-rally. Bradford Council cancelled the last day of the festival for safety reasons. The Council also appealed to the Home Secretary, David Blunkett, and he banned both the BNP and the ANL rallies, though in the event the ANL did hold a demonstration in Centenary Square and supporters of the BNP and other extreme right-wing groups were in evidence in the city centre, particularly in and around public houses in Ivegate and Westgate. Some fighting broke out and a white youth was stabbed. Convinced that the BNP and its ilk were out in force, a large group of Asian young men gathered in mid-afternoon to confront them. Police in riot gear were soon on the scene and before long what was assumed would be a stand-off between Asian youths and the BNP became a violent conflict between Asian youths and the West Yorkshire Police. What happened, therefore, was not really an inter-communal race-riot, as reported in much of the media at the time, but rather an anti-police riot.

The police tactics were to drive the angry crowd away from the city centre, where a good deal of damage had already been done to shops and other properties in Sunbridge Road, Godwin Street, Thornton Road and the adjoining streets. The crowd was then driven further along Westgate and White Abbey Road. But there comes a point where the road rises up Whetley Hill, not far from the junction with Carlisle Road. Here the rioters stood their ground and this was where the worst of the violence was to take place, for the police found it impossible to make progress up the hill. From the late afternoon until the early hours of the next day the police, drawn up in several rows of about thirty officers per row, faced several hundred Asian youths, who pelted them with bricks, stones, petrol bombs and fireworks. Beer kegs were rolled towards the police lines and before long several cars, seized from the nearby Whetley Motor Company, were set alight and trundled down

Derelict Upper Globe public house (key location in the 2001 riot). (Sue Naylor)

the hill. The *Telegraph and Argus* (9 July 2001) gave the following account: 'Cheers and whistles rose up from the mob as a missile hit its target. Seconds later, the wounded officer was carried from the battle line by two colleagues. The jeers were soon lost beneath the deafening thunder of concrete crashing onto riot shields. Another stricken officer limped away from the ranks and then another ...'

The police were hopelessly outnumbered, the nearby Upper Globe public house was ablaze and authorisation was sought for baton rounds (plastic bullets) to be used, though this was not granted, possibly because the West Yorkshire Police chiefs were reluctant for their force to be the first to use such weaponry in mainland Britain. Eventually reinforcements from other police forces – including officers from as far away as Merseyside – arrived to bolster the local police's flagging efforts.

The worst incident of the night concerned Manningham Labour Club, which was fire-bombed and had its doors deliberately blocked so that the twenty-eight people inside were unable to escape. They took refuge in the cellar until they were eventually rescued by the police and fire service. Miraculously, none of them were killed. The club itself was totally destroyed. Rain began to fall some-time after midnight and the rioters gradually began to disperse, though the last incident logged by the police was as late as 10.53 a.m. on 8 July, a report that tools had been looted from a hardware shop with the possibility that these might be used as weapons later in the day. The shop was, incidentally, next door to Lawcroft House police station.

There were other more minor disturbances throughout Bradford in the following few days, including a confrontation on Monday 9 July between white youths and police on the predominantly-white Ravenscliffe estate, an area of run-down council housing in Eccleshill. There were plenty of arrests but nobody was charged with riot, leading to accusations of racism – if you are an Asian you get sent down for riot, but if you are white you get off more lightly. In truth, unpleasant and violent as it was, the Ravenscliffe disturbance was small-beer compared with what had happened at the weekend on the other side of the city.

More than 300 police officers were injured during the riots and fifty-five arrests were made at the time. The police had taken extensive video footage and in the following weeks pictures of rioters appeared in the local press – and this led to many more arrests. In some cases family members contacted the police about the identities of rioters, or even frog-marched culprits to the police station. Eventually a total of 297 arrests were made, 187 people were charged with riot – an unprecedented number in British legal history – and forty-five with violent disorder. A total of 200 jail sentences were handed down; many of those found guilty of riot received five years in prison and Mohammed Ilyas, the man who torched the Manningham Labour Club, received twelve years. In contrast with the mainly youthful rioters, Mohammed Ilyas was aged forty-eight and was described as a businessman.

The cost of the riot was £3.4 million for the police operation and a further £7.4m of damage. However, the long-term damage to Bradford was incalculable. For example, Bradford University had to revise its marketing strategy and concentrate on recruiting local students to its courses once it was realised that students from elsewhere in the UK were reluctant to live and study in a city that was closely associated with violent upheaval and racial discord. And the riots did nothing to help attract much-needed inward investment and business to Bradford; indeed some firms left the city.

However, it is worth considering what might have motivated the rioters. Of course there were some who seized an opportunity to indulge in wanton destruction and looting, but there were no doubt others who genuinely believed that they had to take up arms to defend their neighbourhood – their city – against hostile intruders. A heavy police presence that seemed to be protecting those intruders rather than safe-guarding the local citizenry could quite easily have been perceived as an alien force to be confronted. Three and a half centuries earlier the people of Bradford had felt compelled to take up arms to repel the hostile forces of the Crown, which were intent on capturing the town and imposing their will upon the townspeople (see Chapter Two). The violence of the rioters in 2001 must be condemned, but some of those involved in it may unwittingly have been following in the ancient footsteps of other Bradfordians.

Two months after the Bradford riots New York's World Trade Center was destroyed by Islamic extremists. Bradford's Muslims were reportedly shocked by the act, although some said that they understood what had motivated the

View of where the 2001 riot occurred in White Abbey Road. (Sue Naylor)

perpetrators. The subsequent invasions of Iraq and Afghanistan by American and British forces and the appalling suicide bombings in London in July 2005 did little to promote harmony between Bradford's Muslim citizens and the rest of the populace. Much needed to be done.

Two official reports into community relations in Bradford were published in 2001. One was produced by Lord Ouseley, the Chairman of the Commission for Racial Equality. Ouseley's report contained the following statement: 'deep changes in attitudes and behaviour ... must be achieved across communities to bring about change for all the people of Bradford'. Few could disagree. Ouseley commented that Bradford was essentially a segregated community, something that most people in the city had been well aware of for some time. He also said that there needed to be better partnerships between community groups, improvements in education and reforms to policing. The detail of how all this was to be achieved, however, was left somewhat vague.

Lawcroft House Police Station. (Sue Naylor)

Ted Cantle, a senior government adviser, also produced a report. There was more substance here, for after commenting, like Ouseley, that the root of the problem lay in segregated and polarised communities, Cantle went on to make some quite radical proposals. He suggested that there should be an oath of allegiance that newcomers to Britain should be encouraged to take. Such a proposal would have been dismissed as outrageous if not downright racist just a few years earlier, but at the start of the twenty-first century it met with approval, as did Cantle's proposal that a 'meaningful concept of citizenship' should be promoted in schools and in society generally. His most radical proposal involved ensuring that all schools – independent as well as state – should give at least 25 per cent of their places to pupils from alternative backgrounds. This proposal has yet to be taken up by any of the major political parties in the UK. Cantle also proposed that the police should make more efforts to engage with local communities, while at the same time coming down much more heavily on the drugs gangs that operated in deprived areas.

There were some signs of improvement as the twenty-first century progressed. The police in Bradford had certainly learned valuable lessons from the 2001 riots, as had Bradford Council. So when, in August 2010, the English Defence League (EDL) descended upon Bradford to stage a rally, the police were well prepared and the 700 or so EDL supporters were effectively neutralised by the presence of 1,600 police officers. In addition, a multi-racial peace rally of Bradford's citizens presented a calm and united front against the EDL intrusion. There was very little trouble and certainly nothing to compare with the events which had afflicted the city in 2001, when just the mere rumour of unwelcome visitors had caused a weekend of violent mayhem. And when other towns and cities throughout Britain were subjected to riots and looting in the summer of 2011, Bradford remained peaceful. Perhaps Bradford was beginning to get some things right after all.

fifteen

WHERE NEXT?

Things are done to the people of Bradford rather than for the people of
Bradford.

A resident of Bradford, speaking in 2009

This was a common enough view in the early years of the new millennium. Many people expressed their belief (often through the
letters column of the *Telegraph and Argus* and the *Yorkshire Post*)
that Bradford had suffered from a lack of effective civic leadership possibly stretching back many years. Power was seen as being too often in
the hands of career politicians and senior officers who had only limited knowledge of the city and even less affection for it. For these people Bradford was
merely a project or a stepping-stone towards career advancement elsewhere.
Alan Carling of Bradford University spoke for many; he was quoted in *Common
Sense Regeneration*, published by Bradford Civic Society in 2009:

> As I see it [Bradford] Council faces a difficult situation which is historically
> unprecedented in the UK, or even perhaps in Europe, in combining rapid
> cultural and demographic change with economic transformation and decline.
> The Council has shown a penchant for grandiose schemes planned or executed
> by people from outside the district who are often paid enormous consultancy
> fees ... This amounts to a kind of pathology – an inferiority complex, maybe – in
> which local views and local people count for very little, whereas external experts,
> who know next to nothing about Bradford, are received with rapt attention.

People were well aware, as Ousley and Cantle had said in their reports (see
Chapter Fourteen), that the city had become divided along ethnic lines. The
population in the ring of inner-city wards was, according to the 2001 census,
between 60 and 70 per cent Asian, while the outer suburbs were predominantly

University of Bradford Management Centre, Emm Lane. (Sue Naylor)

National Media Museum. (Sue Naylor)

white. Tong and Wibsey, for example, were both more than 90 per cent white. But Bradford was also deeply divided along economic lines. It contained some of the most economically-deprived areas anywhere, yet some places, such as Ilkley, were among the most prosperous in the entire country. Creating a Bradford-wide sense of community was a forbidding task. And for many years in the late twentieth century the task was viewed as something that should not even be tackled for ideological reasons. The following is a statement published by Bradford Council in 1982, as part of its twelve-point race relations plan: 'Every section of the multi-cultural, multi-racial city has an equal right to maintain its own identity, culture, language, religion and customs.' At first sight this seems perfectly fair and just, but in a city that had such huge discrepancies in terms of prosperity and life-chances, the statement could be seen as an unintended recipe for a form of apartheid.

The Honeyford affair

Ray Honeyford was appointed headmaster of Drummond Middle School in 1980. The school was in the heart of Manningham and the majority of its pupils were from Asian families. In 1984 Honeyford wrote an article entitled *Education and Race – an Alternative View*, which was published in the *Salisbury Review*. In his article Honeyford examined what he believed to be the factors that were hindering the educational performance of his Asian pupils. His argument was that immigrant families should be more in tune with the cultural norms of the majority white community. He also stated that the acquisition of a good standard of English should be a priority for the Asian populace. If these things were neglected, he said, the outlook for many pupils in his school would be bleak. None of this seems particularly contentious in the twenty-first century, but at the time his views were regarded as totally unacceptable by some prominent city councillors and education officers. Their opinion was that promoting the learning of English too vigorously really amounted to linguistic colonialism, while moves to emphasise the British way of life would undermine the cultural heritage of the Asian community.

For some, Honeyford's gravest error was not so much his heretical views but where he had published them. The *Salisbury Review*, edited by Roger Scruton, had an editorial stance which was essentially that of traditional conservatism, as espoused by the third Marquis of Salisbury, Britain's prime minister in the late nineteenth century. It could be said that in choosing this particular vehicle for his views Honeyford was being too politically partisan, something that was inappropriate for the headteacher of a school. The tone of the article, some thought, was patronising and even arrogant. And of course many deemed it highly offensive to the ethnic group that Honeyford was supposed to be serving.

Very soon a campaign was launched to get Honeyford sacked and Drummond Middle School was picketed on a daily basis by a variety of groups – activists from the National Union of Teachers, angry community representatives, offended citizens and so on. After a time an alternative school was set up as part of this campaign and some children were withdrawn from Drummond in order to attend it. Bradford Council dithered. Honeyford was first disciplined, later dismissed, then reinstated and finally persuaded to take early retirement with a pay-off reported to be £70,000, plus an index-linked pension.

The Honeyford affair was highly important because it crystallised the debate about multiculturalism, not just in Bradford but in the rest of the country. Honeyford's opponents believed that his views were a throwback to a less enlightened era when it was assumed that the values, language and culture of the host community were naturally superior to those of more recent arrivals. Some of his opponents no doubt also felt that, as an employee of the Council, it was his duty to abide by its policies, not to go into print and criticise them so publicly.

On the other hand, Honeyford's supporters, while conceding that perhaps he had been naïve and unwise to publish his article in an avowedly right-wing journal, nevertheless felt that some of his views were valid. Immigrant families, they said, had not come to Britain because of the weather; they had settled in places like Bradford in the hope of achieving a more prosperous life. It was the duty of schools to help people to fulfil this aspiration. Equality of opportunity was severely hindered if English language acquisition was soft-pedalled or if people were denied knowledge about Britain's heritage and the British way of life.

By the new millennium this view had generally prevailed and the concept of multiculturalism, as advocated so vehemently by Honeyford's detractors in the 1980s, had largely been abandoned. It was realised that a policy of separate development along ethnic lines was not going to work. Graham Mahoney, the Council's principal race relations officer, summed up the issue in a 2001 report: 'The issue of race is crucial. Given the demographic trends, Bradford as a whole cannot succeed unless its ethnic minority populations prosper.'

Ray Honeyford died in February 2012 at the age of seventy-seven.

International Curry
House. (Sue Naylor)

Morrisons supermarket.
(Sue Naylor)

Centenary Square
development.
(Sue Naylor)

The dark side

The story of Bradford would not be complete without reference to some of the horrifying criminal cases that have, all too often, brought the city a great deal of unwanted publicity. In recent times the city has produced three notorious serial killers.

Donald Neilson, dubbed the Black Panther by the media, was born in Bradford in 1936. He carried out an estimated 400 burglaries before turning to the more lucrative possibilities of armed robbery. Between 1967 and his eventual arrest in 1975 he robbed at least eighteen post offices and murdered three post office employees. In 1975 Neilson kidnapped and murdered seventeen-year-old Lesley Whittle. When interviewed by the police after his arrest, Neilson's wife claimed to know nothing of his life of crime, despite the fact that firearms, ammunition and black leather masks were discovered in the couple's Bradford home. Neilson died in prison in December 2011.

Not long after Neilson was murdering and kidnapping, another serial killer was on the loose. Peter Sutcliffe, the so-called Yorkshire Ripper, was born in Shipley in 1946 and grew up in Bingley. Sutcliffe first came to the attention of the police in 1969 when he assaulted a Bradford prostitute. No charges were brought. Sutcliffe murdered Wilma McCann in Leeds in October 1975. Between that killing and his arrest in January 1981, Sutcliffe murdered at least another ten women in West Yorkshire and two more in Manchester. At first it was thought that he only targeted prostitutes, but after a time it became clear that this was not so. For example, Barbara Leach, who was murdered in September 1979 in Bradford, was a student at Bradford University, and Uphadya Bandara, who survived an attack in Headingley in September 1980, was a doctor doing post-graduate work at Leeds University.

The sheer number of the attacks and their sickening violence created an atmosphere of intense anxiety in Bradford and the other towns and cities of West Yorkshire. This lasted for years. Women were fearful of going out after dark and some even began to wonder if the Ripper might be one of their male relatives or acquaintances.

The police operation to apprehend the Ripper was one of the largest ever undertaken in the UK, at one stage involving 300 police officers. However, the investigation was seriously flawed. Several women who survived attacks were able to give very accurate descriptions of their assailant, but to no avail. Sutcliffe himself was interviewed by the police on nine separate occasions. The

police became convinced that the murderer was not a local man but someone from Sunderland, for they had been sent an audio tape on which the speaker had a Wearside accent. The tape contained a confession together with some mocking criticism of the police's lack of success. Indeed, such was this lack of success that in November 1980 Prime Minister Margaret Thatcher seriously proposed that she should come to Yorkshire to lead the investigation personally. She was dissuaded by her Cabinet colleagues.

As with the Black Panther, the Yorkshire Ripper was eventually captured almost by accident. In January 1981 two officers in Sheffield arrested Sutcliffe, who later confessed to being the Ripper. In May of the same year he was sentenced to life imprisonment for the murder of thirteen women. He may well have killed more. The Byford Report, made public in 2006, contains the following: 'We feel it highly improbable that the crimes in respect of which Sutcliffe has been charged and convicted are the only ones attributable to him.'

In October 2006 John Humble, from Sunderland, was arrested and convicted for sending the hoax tape that had misled the police. He was sent to prison for eight years

After the Black Panther and the Yorkshire Ripper came the self-styled Crossbow Cannibal. Stephen Griffiths, aged forty, was studying for a PhD in criminology at Bradford University; his doctorate dealt with nineteenth-century murders. Between June 2009 and May 2010 Griffiths murdered three Bradford prostitutes. Dismembered body parts of two of the victims were later found in the River Aire at Shipley. No trace of the third was found. Arrested and brought to court, Griffiths referred to himself as the Crossbow Cannibal when asked to give his name. In December 2010 he was given a life sentence, the judge stipulating that there could be no possibility of parole. Griffiths hinted to the police that he had committed other murders.

Keighley became the focus of four murders in 2001 and 2002. These killings were not the work of a serial killer but the result of a turf war between two rival gangs of Asian drug dealers: the Topenders, who controlled the drugs trade in the Highfield Lane area, and the Bottomenders, who operated around Lawkholme Lane. The gangs clearly saw themselves as being in the tradition of Chicago mobsters, the Bottomenders even having a picture of Al Capone displayed on the wall of their headquarters. One of the murders was an execution-style killing of a sixteen-year-old gang member at a petrol station in Haworth Road, Bradford. Another involved the very public murder of Qadir Ahmed, who was ambushed at the busy Victoria Park roundabout in Keighley.

His car was rammed off the road and he was bludgeoned to death as he tried to escape. His murderers were arrested and given long prison sentences. Reported in the *Telegraph and Argus* (27 June 2003), Detective Superintendent Phil Sedgwick commented: 'This brutal crime threw the spotlight on Keighley for the wrong reasons.'

In November 2005 PC Sharon Beshenivsky was shot and killed when responding to a robbery at a travel agent in Morley Street in the centre of Bradford. Three men of Somali background were subsequently given lengthy prison sentences for the crime.

Rebranding Bradford

For the national media, eager for sensational stories, Bradford must have seemed like a godsend, for here was a city that appeared to be producing race-riots, mass-murderers and controversy on a regular basis, all against a backdrop of deprivation, prostitution, gang-warfare and drug problems. Channel Four documentary teams were constantly haunting the city, bent on exploring issues of race, poverty and crime. Many within the city, however, knew that Bradford was a far more complex place than the London-based media realised. Councillor Jeanette Sunderland commented in the *Telegraph and Argus* (5 November 2011), when yet another television documentary was being planned: 'I find [Bradford] one of the most culturally literate places in the country. Sadly a lot of people from outside have a very fixed view of us.'

Clearly a better image was required. In the later decades of the twentieth century and into the new millennium, Bradford Council and the city's business community launched several campaigns aimed at rebranding the city so that it would shed its negative image and – above all – attract more inward investment. One initiative was aimed at promoting the city as a tourist destination. There was a poster campaign featuring photographs of highlights on the tourist trail – steam locomotives chugging along the Worth Valley Railway, Titus Salt's magnificent mausoleum in Saltaire, the Brontë Parsonage at Haworth, and so on, all under the heading 'Bradford, a Surprising Place'.

Another campaign in the 1980s was entitled 'Bradford's Bouncing Back!' which for some reason featured cuddly teddy-bears and one Christmas an inflatable Santa Claus attached to City Hall. Other promotional campaigns came and went. At the start of the new millennium there was '20-20 Vision',

Some of the earliest social housing in Bradford city centre. (Sue Naylor)

Delayed developments in the city centre. (Sue Naylor)

which sought to ensure that by the year 2020 Bradford would be *the* place in which 'to live, learn, work and play'. It was not clear how this was to be achieved within the stated time frame, however. And rather to the surprise of its more cynical citizens, Bradford made a bid to be European Capital of Culture in 2008. The bid failed, and the accolade was eventually bestowed upon Liverpool.

Another strategy employed by the Council to change Bradford's image involved planning prestigious large-scale building projects. Over the course of many years, for example, several elaborate schemes to transform Odsal Stadium into a top national sporting venue were proposed, but they all came to nought. The Council also commissioned Alsop Architects to prepare a masterplan for the development of the city centre. This highly controversial (and expensive) plan, published in 2003, was soon scaled down, partly because funding from the National Lottery failed to materialise. A scheme to build a new shopping centre in Forster Square was launched. Many of the shops and offices that had originally been built in the 1960s were demolished to make way for the centre, but the project stalled and for a number of years all that could be seen was a large empty space.

There were some citizens who felt that Bradford Council was not taking full advantage of some obvious features that could be exploited to promote the city. They pointed to Bradford's well-deserved status as the first UNESCO City of Film and asked why more had not been made of it. Few UK cities could boast a World Heritage site. Bradford had one – Saltaire – yet for a number of years this gem lacked a proper visitors' centre. Some people also felt that assets such as Bradford University's excellent School of Management and its internationally renowned Peace Studies Department were not given sufficient prominence when the city was being showcased to the wider world.

By 2013 it seemed to many of the more jaundiced citizens of Bradford that the Council's propensity for producing grandiose schemes and elaborate promotional campaigns was often little more than desperate window-dressing. But others were cautiously optimistic, believing, in particular, that if more developments in the city centre, such as City Park (opened in March 2012), could be completed it might indeed attract inward investment; and Bradford might then turn the corner.

And there were other shafts of light among the dark clouds of pessimism. Some Bradford-based businesses flourished, the obvious example being Morrisons, which had grown from a stall in Rawson Market to become by 2011 Britain's fourth largest supermarket chain, with over 450 branches throughout

Science lesson at Belle Vue Girls' School. (Sue Naylor)

the country. The Yorkshire Building Society, with its headquarters in Bradford, was the second largest building society in the UK by 2011, with assets of £20 billion. A number of Asian businesses also enjoyed success. For example, Mumtaz, which started life as a small restaurant in Great Horton Road, had become an internationally-known food and restaurant brand by the early twenty-first century, and the highly successful Aagrah restaurant chain was opening branches throughout Yorkshire. In total Bradford's economy was worth £7 billion by 2011, greater therefore than the economies of either Leicester or Nottingham. And those who voted for the controversial Respect politician, George Galloway, in spring 2012 presumably believed that was a step in the right direction too.

The future

Bradford has some unique features and traditions, which with astute handling could lead to a resurgence of prosperity and influence. One of the most important features is the city's age profile. Unlike most other places in the UK, Bradford does not have an aged population – quite the reverse. Having a lot of young people around means that there is an energy about the place. If this energy can be connected to forward-looking civic leadership, then there is a chance that an upsurge in legitimate entrepreneurial activity will provide the basis for long-term economic growth. A particularly welcome development has been the number of well-educated young women from Bradford's Asian communities who are now employed throughout the city in numerous firms and organisations. This is in sharp contrast with the situation only a few years ago when education and careers were not seen to be particularly important for Asian women. Perhaps the future of Bradford is in their hands.

The city has a fine stock of Victorian buildings that managed to escape the demolition contractor's hammer in the 1960s. It is only comparatively recently that planners and politicians have realised what an invaluable boon they are to the city, if they are sensitively modernised and put to new uses. Bradford is indeed a surprising place and the cityscape reflects that, as do the large tracts of dramatic and beautiful countryside that are only a short distance from the city centre.

The challenge in the new millennium, therefore, is for Bradford to use its considerable assets wisely and well so that it can re-assert and re-invent itself as a prosperous and – above all – a self-confident community. Despite current economic uncertainties many of the other great Victorian cities of the North – notably Manchester and Leeds – are already well on the way to achieving this. Bradford can do the same.

BIBLIOGRAPHY

Aronsfeld, C.C., *German Jews in 19th Century Bradford* (Yorkshire Archaeological Journal, Vol. 53, 1981)

Bellerby, Rachel, *Chasing the Sixpence; the lives of Bradford mill folk* (Fort Publishing, 2005)

Bilton, Michael,*Wicked Beyond Belief* (Harper Perennial, 2006)

Bradford Art Galleries and Museums (ed.), *The Face of Worstedopolis,* (Bradford Art Galleries and Museums, 1982)

Bradford Civic Society, *Common Sense Regeneration* (2009)

Bradford Library Service (ed.), *The Siege of Bradford* (Bradford Library Service, date unknown)

Burne and Young, *The Battle of Adwalton Moor* (unpublished essay, Bradford Library Service, 1959)

Bujra, Janet and Pearce, Jenny, *Saturday Night and Sunday Morning, the 2001 Bradford riot and beyond* (Vertical Editions, 2011)

Cudworth, William, *Historical Notes on the Bradford Corporation* (Thomas Brear, 1881)

Cudworth, William, *Round About Bradford* (1874. Republished by Mountain Press, 1968)

Cudworth, William, *Worstedopolis: A sketch history of the town and trade of Bradford* (1888, republished by The Old Bradfordian Press, 1997)

Duckett, B (ed.), *The German Immigrants; their influence in 19th Century Bradford* (Propagator Press, 2007)

Duckett, B and Waddington-Feather, J, *Bradford, History & Guide* (Tempus, 2005)

Ellison, D.B., *Bradford on the Eve of the Civil War* (unpublished essay, Bradford Library Service)

Fieldhouse, Joseph, *Bradford* (Longman, 1972)

Firth, Gary, *A History of Bradford* (Phillimore, 1997)

Firth, Gary, *J.B. Priestley's Bradford* (Tempus, 2006)

Firth, Paul, *Four Minutes to Hell* (Parrs Wood Press, 2005)

Greenhalf, Jim, *It's a Mean Old Scene; a history of modern Bradford from 1974* (Redbeck Press 2003)

Hird, Horace, *Bradford Remembrancer* (McDonald Book Co. Ltd, 1972)

Holdsworth, Peter, *The Rebel Tyke; Bradford and J.B. Priestley* (Bradford Libraries, 1994)

Holroyd, Abraham (ed.), *Collecteana Bradfordiana* (1878)

James, David, *Bradford* (Ryburn Publishing, 1990)

James, John, *History of Bradford* (Longmans, 1866. Republished by Morten, 1973)

James, John, *History of the Worsted Manufacture in England* (1857. Republished by Cass and Co. 1968)

Jowitt J.A., *Textiles and Society in Bradford and Lawrence, USA, 1880-1920* (The Bradford Antiquary, Vol. 5, 1991)

Leach, Peter and Pevsner, Nikolaus, *The Buildings of England; Yorkshire West Riding, Leeds, Bradford and the North* (Yale UP, 2009)

McMillan, Margaret, *The Life of Rachel McMillan* (Dent, 1927)

Parker, B.J.R (and others, ed.), *Education in Bradford 1870-1970* (Educational Services Committee, Bradford Corporation, 1970)

Pearce, Cyril, *The Manningham Mills Strike* (University of Hull, 1975)

Pratt, Michael, *The Influence of the Germans on Bradford* (unpublished essay, Margaret McMillan College, Bradford, 1971)

Priestley, J.B., *English Journey* (Heinemann, 1934)

Raw, David, *Bradford Pals* (Pen and Sword, 2006)

Reynolds, Jack, *Saltaire* (Bradford Art Galleries and Museums, 1976)

Richardson, C, *The Bradford Region* (Bradford Libraries, Archives and Information Service, 2002)

Richardson, C, *Irish Settlement in mid-19th Century Bradford,* (Yorkshire Bulletin of Economic and Social Research, Vol. 20, No. 1, 1968)

Richardson, C, *The Irish in Victorian Bradford,* (Bradford Antiquary, Part xlv, 1971)

Sheeran, George, *The Buildings of Bradford* (Tempus, 2005)

Suddards, Roger (ed.), *Titus of Salt* (Watmough, 1976)

Taylor, Simon and Gibson, Kathryn, *Manningham: Character and Diversity in a Bradford Suburb* (English Heritage, 2010)

Wolfe, Humbert, *Now A Stranger* (Cassell, 1933)

Woods, Mike and Platts, T. (eds), *Bradford in the Great War* (Sutton, 2007)